SO YOU WANT
TO BE A LIBRARIAN

Other Books in This Series

So You Want to Be a Librarian

by SARAH LESLIE WALLACE

HARPER & ROW, PUBLISHERS

NEW YORK AND EVANSTON

020.69
W/5

FIRST EDITION

B—N

LIBRARY OF CONGRESS CATALOG CARD NUMBER: 63-8219

To
Dorothy
who has put up with my uncertain schedule
and equally uncertain disposition during
the writing of this book

Contents

Introduction

WHEN I WAS A CHILD in grade school I lived over a mile from the nearest branch of the public library, but distance made no difference. During the school year I went to the library several times a week, coming home with books which I often read before the evening was over. In vacation periods my brother and sister and I would either hike around the lake to the branch or load up the baskets of our bicycles and pedal through the park, up and down some steep hills, to return our books and get more. I remember those hills vividly for my bike had no brakes and, if I hoped to avoid a spill, I had to pedal backwards when I went down one.

Sometimes the whole family would climb into the car and all of us would go to the library in style. That was a special event, enjoyed from beginning to end.

The high school I attended had a library which I used but once or twice. Across the street was another branch of the public library to which I gravitated. I especially remember a highly romantic tale called, I think, *Lady Peggy Goes to Town*, which caused my downfall in study hall. I was quiet enough, deep in my book, but evidently Lady Peggy did not look as serious in her blue buckram covers as I thought, or else the teacher was suspicious of any student so buried in study. Whatever it was, she descended upon my unsuspecting head and strongly suggested that I exchange Lady Peggy for something in the line of geometry or grammar.

Until I went to college, a library was a place where one found wonderful absorbing, adventurous stories. Its place in helping me with my lessons, its place in supplying information, never entered my mind.

I was one of those who augmented a scholarship with work to pay my way through college. The work was in the library where I shelved books, marked books, and collated books, to pay my fees. All the time I was absorbing a knowledge of the breadth and depth of the world of books. But it was not until I graduated from college that I decided I wanted to be a librarian. So, the next fall I headed back to library school to combine my student experience and my interest in books with some knowledge of libraries.

My first job was as a reference librarian in a public library and there I really learned for the first time the adventure and the fun of working with people who want books, who read books, who need books.

Thus I came to the library field through a gradual process. No one told me beforehand of the many roads open to a librarian, of the kind of training he should get, or of the costs and the rewards. It is to help you find out some of these things in advance that this book has been written. It will not answer all your questions. Librarians and libraries are too individual for that. This very individuality is one of the things which makes libraries interesting and which keeps them an uncounted force in our democracy.

The book will, I hope, introduce you to the field. It will

show you where to go for more information and, what is sometimes most important, it will indicate the questions you should ask. Try to see many kinds of libraries and talk to many kinds of librarians. I have shown you that I did not think to use my high school library because no one ever really took the trouble to tell me what I might find there. Now you will be introduced to your school library and taught how to use it as part of your curriculum. If you are thinking of a library career, however, you should not be satisfied with this alone. Get acquainted with your school librarian. See if you can work as a student volunteer. Visit libraries when you are traveling. This is the best way to wipe stereotypes from your mind and substitute instead the actual variety to be found in buildings, collections, and staff.

Continue your explorations in college. By this time, if you are wise, you will have chosen your vocational field, but learn about libraries with your own eyes and ears as well as through your formal courses.

No one who opens the newspaper to see the articles about manned orbital flights, rockets to the moon, the use of atomic energy in curing cancer, or the latest development in hydro-gen bombs needs to be told that the world is moving faster and faster. This speed is not confined to science alone. It touches all fields. Therefore, the information you find in this book will be constantly changing also. In it you will find clues as to where you should look for recent developments. Heed these clues. If you are to be a good librarian you will learn to verify sources by looking in more than one place.

What never changes is the fun of being a librarian. No other profession can offer the constant change and interest, the chance to be on the edge of all professions. Librarians could know what is going on in the world even though they might never open a newspaper or listen to a radio. For instance, a public librarian at the end of a day would know from requests coming in by telephone and over the desk:

That the women's symphony association was planning a ball with a Louis XIV theme—this because of requests from the decorations committee for materials on Versailles and from the costume committee for pictures of French court dress during the seventeenth century;

That the debate question for the year is federal aid to education—the onslaught of high school students for material is proof;

That a local firm is seeking new markets in South America—a team from the company has been combing the business directories of the large cities there;

That the director of Health, Education and Welfare has been invited to be the speaker at the dedication of the new high school—the committee chairman wanted to know how to address a letter to him;

That Mrs. Brown is having trouble with her sixteen-year-old boy—she asked if the library had any material on how to regulate teen-age use of the family car;

That two rugged young men are opening a north woods resort—their request for cabin building, advertising, and state laws governing hotels and resorts is an indication;

That Mr. Winters is well along with his book on the early days of the theater in the state—the librarians have been at work all year assisting him in finding names, dates and other facts;

That the mutual savings bank is going to run a series of ads on people famous for their thrift, beginning with Benjamin

Franklin—the agency handling the account sought the library's help;

That a national advertising campaign on strawberry shortcake will soon appear in the magazines—the city's big flour mill wanted to know when strawberries would be on the market in most places in the United States;

That the lieutenant-governor died unexpectedly during the night—the newspaper has called to verify biographical data.

And so it goes through the librarian's day.

In the same way, the school librarian knows what is going on in the school, what the teachers are assigning, the hobbies of both teachers and students, the principal's concerns, and the theme for the senior dance. The special librarian knows what projects are being undertaken in his company, what research is being done in new fields, what problems have been encountered.

And every librarian will tell you that there is no thrill equal to that of locating the needed information or the needed book for the person who has asked you for it; the thrill of coming on a long-sought answer; the thrill of knowing that you have supplied a piece which will help to build something, whether it be a life, a business, an education—or a small boy's stamp collection.

Anyone who chooses a profession chooses a responsibility. He must give as well as take. John F. Kennedy's words, spoken on his inauguration as President of the United States, have been quoted often because they are so apt: ". . . ask not what your country can do for you—ask what you can do for your country." This holds true of anything you do. In a profession you profit by the work of those who preceded you. When you choose that path you must think also of those who follow and so bring new vigor, seek new horizons, establish higher goals.

Librarianship can be a great profession. It deals with a great phenomenon: man's thoughts packaged in words. William Hazlitt said: "Words are the only things that last forever; they are more durable than the eternal hills."

May you be happy with words, the words of the great and the thoughtful; may you bring those thoughts to others so that new thought may be generated, and truth expressed in new words.

ONE CANNOT FINISH a book of this type without realizing the debt owed to others for their assistance. The author would like to express appreciation to the librarians who have supplied information and personal experiences for use here. Special mention must be made of the interest and help given by colleagues in the Minneapolis Public and Hennepin County Libraries.

S.L.W.

ONE

What Is a Librarian?

IT ALL HAPPENED on the same morning.
Mary Adams settled herself on the yellow hassock. The
warm spring sun beamed through the windows of the children's room and edged her hair with gold. It highlighted
the thirty expectant faces of the first grade class seated
cross-legged on the floor in front of her. She opened the big
book on her lap and turned it so they could see the brightly
colored pictures as she began the story: "Once upon a
time. . . ."

John Standish laid down his pencil with a sigh. One last
time he had checked the columns of figures on the annual
amounts needed to finance the five-year $3 million building
program the library was submitting to the city council's
capital long-range improvements committee. John had put
all of his knowledge and experience into this proposal for a
new central library and three regional branches. The trustees
had backed his judgment with an enthusiasm they seldom
displayed when voting to spend money. He slid the sheets
into a folder along with the charts and architectural plans
which illustrated the project. As he left the office he paused

15

at his secretary's desk.

"Wish me luck," he said. "If I can convince the conservatives of the need, the rest of the council will vote for it. And that will mean that at last we are on our way to a new central building." He looked around the crowded, file-filled alcove which served as reception room as well as office. "They *must* see it!" The big folder crackled in protest as his hand tightened on it. "How can we serve that city out there with a library built a hundred years ago for a frontier town?" He laughed a little self-consciously. "I should save the speech for the council."

Betty Bradley picked up the house phone and rang the chief of her company's engineering department. "The library has just received a new article on air conditioning, Mr. Danvers. It's a detailed report of the experiments at the university conducted by Professor Herzog. We thought it might help you on the Hallowell job. Would you like to have it sent to you?"

The red-haired boy had not yet become accustomed to his sudden height. He draped it across the desk and opened his battered notebook. A wide grin spread across his face in answer to Ann Stotesbury's welcoming smile. She gave him a mock bow: "I hear your team won the debate with Central High. That's five in a row, isn't it? And all due to your excellent research department!" They both chuckled. Ann went on: "I don't mind telling you that last one on space law almost threw me. That's a subject Thomas Jefferson high school library isn't too strong in, believe me. What's the topic for the next one?"

Her eyes grew serious as they bent over the notebook while

the boy explained his angular handwriting. She nodded in appreciation as he explained his ideas for the brief, then asked him what he had already done to locate information.

"Good," she approved. "Now, I remember there was a good speech on this by Senator Stallard. I'll find it in the Congressional Record. Then, we've started to take a new magazine . . ." She moved about quickly, gathering special materials for this boy who might some day be a senator himself.

Bob McGowan listened sympathetically to the worried woman across the desk. She had spilled blueberries on her best linen tablecloth and was afraid the stain would not come out. He smiled reassuringly and pulled a big red book from the shelf behind him. "This is the best thing we have on removing spots and stains," he told her, turning to the proper page. "I hope it works for you."

Alice Kent opened the patient's door carefully and looked in. The man in the high hospital bed was awake and beckoned to her to come in. "It looks as if I'll be here for quite a while, the doctor says," he told Alice. "I'll need more books like the one you left yesterday. I always did like a good mystery. And say," he added, "if I'm going to be here for as long as they think I will, I might as well find out something about archeology. I always wanted to, but I never had time. When I was a youngster I even thought I might be an archeologist some day but I turned out to be an automobile dealer instead." He cocked an eyebrow at Alice. "Do you think you could locate a good book on it? I'd like to start out in Greece or Egypt."

Jean Lennon put on a little more lipstick and nodded approvingly at herself in the mirror. Then she picked up her books and walked into the studio waving at the crew busy with lights, cameras, and microphones. The television show would go on in twenty minutes. The producer walked over to her. He looked worried. "Hello, Jean," he greeted her. "What are you doing today?" He tipped his head so as to read the titles of the books in her hand. Jean handed one of them to him, opening the other at a brilliant color spread. "Two gorgeous new travel books on Italy," she answered. "Look, isn't this beautiful?" "Beautiful," he echoed abstractedly. "Listen, Jean, we're on a spot. One of the other guests can't get here; his car broke down in some forsaken hole a hundred miles from nowhere. Can you fill fifteen minutes instead of the usual ten?" Jean nodded, laughing. "Don't worry, Ed. You know me when I start talking about books. You'll have to shut me up by force."

George Thompson had the door open almost as soon as the bookmobile drew to a stop: "Could you get your pump working, Mr. Harrison?" he called to the tall, thin man in overalls hurrying across the yard. The farmer shook his head. "No, darned if I know what's wrong. My boy and I have been working on it since five o'clock this morning." George tapped the green pamphlet in his hand. "We got your call just before we started out. This is a government document which should help you spot the trouble. Karl Schumacher on County Road 18 swears by it. He has a pump like yours."

Yes, it all happened on the same morning, and all of them —John, Mary, Betty, Ann, Bob, Alice, Jean, George—were librarians going about the daily excitement of bringing people and books together.

Heritage

Kings, monks, scholars, tyrants, queens, patriots, millionaires—all these are your professional forebears when you become a librarian. Throughout their long and colorful history, libraries have been the preoccupation of the great and wise who saw in them a means of preserving that intangible product of the human mind—ideas.

Among the earliest libraries of which we have any record is a collection of Babylonian clay tablets, dating from as early as 2000 B.C. The keepers of these early Babylonian libraries were called "men of the written tablets."

Assyrians were neighbors to the Babylonians in the ancient world. A library is known to have existed there as early as the eighth century B.C. in the reign of Sargon II. His grandson, King Assurbanipal, who ruled from 668 to 626 B.C., is the one who organized it and enlarged it. Housed in his palace at Nineveh, the collection grew to about 22,000 clay tablets which included works on subjects still found in libraries today—history, astronomy, and mathematics, as examples. There is evidence that the volumes were classified and arranged by subject.

Scholars believe that Egyptian libraries were as old as those of Babylonia, the earliest ones being housed in temples under the care of priests. Because the Babylonians and Assyrians used clay tablets, their collections survived the centuries better than the more fragile papyrus manuscripts of the Egyptians. Also, since the earliest libraries of Egypt were largely archives, their neighbors in Assyria may have produced the first *real* library.

Osymandyas of Egypt is said to be one of the earliest Egyptian kings to have a library of any note. He established a collection of sacred literature. Over the door he placed the inscription: "Here is medicine for the mind."

The early Egyptian names for their libraries are curious and thought-provoking to us. In Thebes, in the ruins of the temple at Karnak, there was found the inscription: "House of Books." Nearby were the tombs of two librarians, father and son, for the office was hereditary.

At Idfu, the library was called the "House of Papyrus" and from a catalog carved in the stone walls we know that it contained books on religion, hunting, astrology, and astronomy.

The most famous library of the ancient world, one which attracted scholars from far and wide was the one at Alexandria. Founded near the close of the fourth century B.C., it is believed to have grown to a collection of 700,000 rolls. Often referred to as the twin libraries of Alexandria because the larger part of the library was housed in the museum and a smaller collection at the Serapeum, a temple to Jupiter-Serapis, its staff numbered more than forty scholar-librarians. Ptolemy—ruler of Egypt—was assiduous in the collection of manuscripts, seeking out the sacred books of the Chaldeans, the Egyptians, and the Romans, and having them translated into Greek for the library. The Septuagint, the pre-Christian version of the Old Testament, was completed here by seventy scholars.

Most of this great collection was destroyed in wars between the Egyptians and the Romans. Julius Caesar burned part of it in 47 B.C. Historians differ as to its final fate, but the entire library was destroyed or scattered whether by Aurelian, Theodosius the Great, or Caliph Omar. Its loss was a tragedy, not only to the people of that day but to those of succeeding centuries.

Less than a century after the Alexandrian library was founded, Attalus I established one at Pergamum in Asia Minor. It rivaled its predecessor in size, receiving as a single gift some 200,000 volumes sent by Mark Antony to Cleopatra to replace some of those destroyed by Caesar at Alexandria. It is said that there was such rivalry between the two libraries that Egypt placed an embargo on the shipment of papyrus to Pergamum, hoping thus to cripple the growth of its library. To offset this loss Pergamum developed parchment as a substitute.

The Romans were more interested in wars than in books. They brought back their first libraries as spoils from the countries they conquered. However, Julius Caesar seems to have planned to establish a library for the public, a plan his adopted son Augustus carried out. Later emperors followed suit until by 300 A.D. Rome boasted thirty public libraries. In fact, the growth of both public and private libraries was so healthy throughout the balance of the life of the Roman Empire that historians have rated the facilities of this period as better than those of the mid 1700's.

The Roman libraries were well organized. Busts of the various writers projected from the sections housing their works. Attention was given to colors and decorations which would be conducive to rest, reading, and study. The palatine library had a librarian in charge of Latin books and one in charge of Greek books. We know that there were several grades of workers. There was an administrator or procurator who concerned himself with the acquisition of materials and in the administration of the library. There were "bibliotheca" who cared for the books. Since there were several types of "bibliotheca," we know that even then there was specialization in libraries. A "librarius" was a transcriber or copyist.

Women were sometimes engaged in this role.

When the barbarians swept over Europe in the fifth century, most of the Roman libraries were ransacked. Some of the religious manuscripts found their way to monasteries and were preserved. The surviving secular literature was transferred to Constantinople.

During the Middle Ages the importance of books and learning seemed forgotten except in monasteries. The Benedictine monks established the first monastic library in the abbey at Monte Cassino in Italy in 530 A.D. Every new monastery established after that included a library. Printing would not be invented for many centuries—not until about 1450—so in each monastic library a room was set aside where manuscripts were copied by hand. Other religious orders— the Augustinians, the Dominicans, the Franciscans—were also active in gathering manuscripts, in copying, and in translating them. To these libraries and to the monks who built them, who labored long, hunched over desks in these poorly lighted and often cold scriptoria, the world owes the preservation of much of the Greek and Latin literature we have today.

With the coming of the Renaissance and a reawakened interest in learning, others began to collect and to copy manuscripts; and private libraries were built by kings and noblemen. Many of these became the foundations of the famous European libraries of today.

In France, the three sons of John II—Charles V; John, Duke of Berre; and Philip the Bold, Duke of Burgundy— were avid collectors. Charles employed a full-time librarian who cataloged his collection. Indeed, the Bibliothèque Nationale, which now numbers between five and six million books, was built around his library.

Across the Alps in Italy, the search for classical literature was stimulated by such scholars as Petrarch and Boccaccio. The wealthy and powerful Este and Medici families gathered famous collections, Cosimo de' Medici founding a library about 1440 in the cloisters of San Marco which became Italy's first public library.

Although a papal library had existed in the very early centuries of Christianity, the present great Vatican library was founded in 1447 under Pope Nicholas V who had once been a librarian, and who had cataloged the Medici library at San Marco. Five centuries later, another pope, Pius XI, also was a librarian before ascending Peter's throne.

About 1450 John Gutenberg's invention of printing with movable type produced the great 42-line Bible, which even today is still one of the most beautiful books to come from a press. With his invention came the beginning of modern libraries in Europe.

However, in England the effect was slower. It was 150 years before the first great modern library was begun there, with the establishment of the Bodleian Library at Oxford in 1602 by Sir Thomas Bodley, replacing earlier collections destroyed by fire.

The famed British Museum which draws scholars from all over the world was established in 1753. Again, this library had its beginnings in the art collection of Sir Hans Sloane which he willed to the nation. This collection was combined with that of King George II and the Harleian and Cottonian libraries under the now hallowed name of "British Museum."

In the same period, Catherine the Great of Russia confiscated the libraries of a Polish noble family, the Zaluskis, marking the real beginning of Russia's national public library. Formerly the Imperial Public Library, it is now the

Leningrad National Public Library. In its collection are the libraries of the famous French writers, Voltaire and Diderot. The huge All-Union Lenin Public Library at Moscow began in the palace of an eighteenth century nobleman, facing the Kremlin. It is now the center of library activities in the U.S.S.R.

Across the Atlantic, in the small English colonies appearing in the New World, books had their place, too. The first library to be established was the one at Harvard, founded in 1638, when John Harvard bequeathed his collection of 3,500 books to the six-year-old college. In 1656 Captain Robert Keayne willed his library to Boston for public use, also thoughtfully providing funds for a building to house it. Back in England the need for books in these new settlements was not forgotten. Dr. Thomas Bray, who had established English parish libraries, collected 2,500 books from church libraries and sent them to Trinity parish in New York where they were used by both the clergy and the public.

In Philadelphia a group of young working men, which included Benjamin Franklin, met regularly for discussion. They brought their own books to consult during their conferences, as well as to share with each other. "Some inconveniences occurring," as Franklin said, "they all took their books home again." Franklin then embarked on his "first project of a public nature," the organization of a subscription library. He secured fifty subscribers, each of whom contributed forty shillings at the outset and ten shillings a year for fifty years. This Library Company of Philadelphia, founded in 1731, became the pattern for many such libraries throughout the colonies; and Franklin is frequently called the founder of the public library in this country.

As early as 1800 the infant Congress of the newly formed
United States appropriated money for the purchase of books,
and in 1802 a room in the capitol was designated a "library."
Intended as a legislative library for the Congress, the collection was burned by the British in 1814. However, a better
library emerged, for Thomas Jefferson offered to sell his
own library at cost to replace the lost books. In 1815, therefore, 6,700 volumes were procured for $23,950. Again in
1851 the library was swept by fire and only 20,000 books were
saved. Once more bad fortune turned to good. The Smithsonian library was added to the collection, and the United
States began to have a true national library, one which now
numbers over 11 million books.

The American public library system owes much to men
who made fortunes in the growing country, and who used
large shares of these fortunes to make books available to their
fellowmen. There was John Jacob Astor whose millions came
from the fur trade and from his large real estate holdings in
New York City; there was James Lenox, a modest, retiring
man, the son of a Scotch merchant, who loved books, music,
paintings, and gems, whose property, soon to be surrounded
by New York City, attained a fabulous value; there was
Samuel Tilden, New York lawyer, who fought Tammany
Hall and lost the Presidency of the United States by decision
of the electoral commission.

Astor wished to show his gratitude to New York, the city
in which he lived so long and where he fared so well. He left
$400,000 to found a library, hiring Dr. Joseph Green Cogs-
well as well to find "curious, rare and beautiful" books for it.
Lenox, who for years had filled his home with rare and beautiful books, some twenty-two years later in 1870, donated a
smaller but popular reference library. In 1886 Tilden left

half of his estate—a sum of $3 million—as well as his collec-
tion of about 20,000 volumes to found a free public library
for the city. The three funds were merged in 1895 to become
the great New York Public Library.

Born in Dumferline, Scotland, Andrew Carnegie came to
this country when he was only thirteen. Starting to work at
$1.20 a week in a cotton factory, he became one of the world's
richest men. Before his death Carnegie gave away $43 mil-
lion for the establishment of libraries throughout the world.
Another $30 million has been expended since his death. At
the outset, the money was used chiefly for library buildings.
Since 1926, however, the Carnegie Corporation funds have
gone chiefly for professional training of librarians, for en-
larging the resources of college and university libraries, and
for furthering international library cooperation.

Carnegie wrote: "The thing I enjoy most about my books
is that they work day and night. There isn't an hour of the
day all over the world that thousands are not reading those
books, and will always be reading them, and sometimes when
I feel a little vain, I say, 'and I am their teacher.' "

Peter Cooper was another man who followed the rags-to-
riches road and used his wealth to make books available to
his fellowmen. Young Peter, at seventeen, went to work as an
apprentice to a coachbuilder for twenty-five dollars a year,
plus his board. Amassing a fortune in glue, he turned his
golden touch to iron, making the first structural iron for
fireproof buildings. In 1859 he established Cooper Union, a
school for working people. The "reading room" in the school
was stocked with magazines, newspapers, and books designed
to attract workers. It was the only library in New York at
that time which was open at night, its hours being long—
8 A.M. to 10 P.M. The library was well used, three thousand
people patronizing it in its first year.

Dependent at first upon the gifts of public-spirited men or upon the funds they pooled in association and subscription libraries, the American people have recognized the need for books and as the nation has grown, they have taxed themselves to build and maintain the public, school, and state university libraries which spread over the entire country. A country which believes in universal education, and which depends for its existence on an informed electorate must have a flourishing system of libraries.

These are your ancestors—the ancient kings, the patient monks, the great philosophers and scholars, the merchant princes, the modern self-made business barons. When you enter the library profession you join the ranks of those men who, throughout the ages, believed in the importance of ideas, the power in the thoughts of great minds, which have been set down on paper for others to read, to test, and to use.

The Job

Today's library offers more than a splendid heritage, however. It offers a splendid future. The pharaohs and the kings, the merchant princes and the millionaires, the Babylonian "men of the written tablets" and the Roman "bibliotheca" have been followed by modern men and women, equally dedicated, equally courageous, equally visionary. Librarians have, above all, an opportunity to serve their fellowmen. The rapidly expanding body of knowledge, the challenges, ideas, and speculations—some true and some false—which are hurled at men, make it imperative that they find proof, substantiate facts, acquire background, before they commit themselves to the attack or defense of a theory.

One of the roles of a librarian is to select information which the public needs, then to organize it in a system where facts may be easily located. Knowledge has become so special-

ized that even the scholar needs a guide to find his way
around a strange field.

Guiding the uninitiated through the wilderness of print is
also the librarian's job. Like the trained woodsman, he must
show the tenderfoot the signs which put him on the right
trail—signs found in card catalogs and indexes instead of
the moss on the tree and the star in the sky.

There is fun in books, too—escape from this humdrum
world into worlds of adventure, worlds of beauty, worlds of
exploration.

One librarian who, during her career, has been head of a
children's department, chief of a busy neighborhood branch,
and is now in command of the extension department of a
large city library, did not think twice when asked what made
her become a librarian.

"I thought it would be fun," she answered. She stopped to
consider, then added, "And it has been."

This is the reward of a librarian who knows the pure enjoyment to be found in books, and how to share it with those
who come to him for guidance. He grows in the knowledge of
books and the knowledge of people. He knows the joy of
bringing them together, of giving the right book to the
right man at the right time.

Would You Be a Good Librarian?

Lawrence Clark Powell, eminent librarian, author, and
bibliophile, says that once when he asked what to look for in
a good librarian he was told by a veteran: "Good feet."

There are times when almost any librarian would wearily
agree, but in other circumstances they would list other
qualifications first.

Librarians are people—many different kinds of people

doing many different kinds of work. By that token there are many different skills, attributes, and personality factors found among them. Also, since librarians are people, living among other people, it goes without saying that there is not a single desirable personality trait which would not be desirable in a librarian. However, as in most professions, there are certain qualities which a person considering librarianship as a lifework should look for in himself.

First, of course, he should love books and reading since his life will be spent with books, among other people who love books, and serving people who want what is in books. He must read because he must know his product, be able to satisfy his customer. It is knowledge of what lies behind the cover that enables the librarian to help the sad-faced woman who says her husband has died and she needs to find new outlets, new paths for her thoughts. That same knowledge recalls just the right book for the man who likes stories about Africa. Over and over, a hundred times a day in a hundred different ways, the things you have read can be used to meet the needs of the people of all ages and sizes who come to the library.

Underlying this love of books, in fact an integral part of it, is a respect for great and good ideas and a desire to see them shared by others through the printed word.

With this love of books must go a love of people. The librarian must be interested in people, interested enough to discover their wants and needs even when they themselves are inarticulate. When a shy young man, twisting his hat in his hands, asks for books on psychology, the good librarian is understanding and does not send for a popular text on the subject. He probes gently until the young man admits that what he really wants is something to help him be popular with girls. And he hands him a good book on personality development.

The librarian must be interested in serving others, in sharing his knowledge, and in putting the skills of his profession at the service of others. The librarian often knows how to get at the information which others—scientists, engineers, teachers, authors, businessmen, artists—will put to work. Even librarians who do not work "at the desk," who are in areas not approached directly by the public, must have this love of people. Those who are engaged in the selection and acquisition of books must *understand* books and people because they must *understand and care* about what readers like, and they must have a desire to get it to them. Catalogers and classifiers must *understand* how people's minds work and so arrange and index the collection that the library user can locate his materials easily. And every librarian, whether he works directly with the reader or not, must work with those around him, his fellow staff members. The job of each will be better done if they like and understand each other.

Service will be better, the staff will work better together, the public will be better satisfied, if the librarian has tact. In the final analysis, tact is a basic courtesy and respect for others which is essential to harmonious human relations. Every day the librarian must meet and serve many types of people—many races, many nationalities, and many ages. He works with men and women of varying educational backgrounds, with a wide spread of intellectual levels, with an equally wide spread of economic levels. He must help the inarticulate, the shy, and the timorous as well as the glib, the forward, and the proud. Each must be met with equal respect and served to his satisfaction. This satisfaction comes from the way in which he is served as well as the materials he is given. Yes, you must have tact to be a good librarian.

Libraries are only a mass of books, papers, magazines, and pictures which are completely unusable unless they are arranged in a logical order and kept in that order. Indexes must be developed and kept up to date to act as keys to the information contained in them. Because of this, accuracy and a sense of order are helpful attributes for a librarian. They are essential if he works with others, for the collection and the records must always be in order so that every staff member knows where things are and how to find them. The librarian who knew every book in his collection and where it was shelved from some personal index kept in his head has gone with high button shoes. He was buried in the tremendous output of print. Today's librarian needs not only mechanical devices, indexes and catalogs, but he needs also other human beings to work with him. One misplaced word, one misfiled card, one book shelved in the wrong place can mean that some man or woman may not find a needed fact that, in some cases, would have changed his or her future.

Elizabeth Morrow has a Christmas story about a little girl who discovers her mother's rueful wish for a "quart of judgment" and tries to find one to give her. She asks for a definition of judgment and confusing "sense" for "cents" she presents her mother with a pint—all she could save—of copper pennies. Librarians need at least a pint and could often wish for a bushel of judgment. Like the man who had to sort potatoes all day, they are faced with decisions, decisions—and judgment is needed to make good ones. Judgment is needed in hiring a staff and using its skills to the best advantage. Judgment is needed in planning the library's services; in expending the budgeted funds to the best advantage. It is needed in making wise regulations and even more in knowing when to break and when to keep them.

Librarians are subject to many pressures. Some have lost their positions over matters of judgment, particularly in the selection of books. They often handle large sums, not only for the operation of a system but for the purchase of equipment or the construction of buildings. It takes wisdom and balance to expend money which is not your own so that it will bring the best results and the greatest return to those who have entrusted it to you. Librarians must recommend policies to their boards of trustees. These must be well conceived and well timed. Library administrators—whether they head large institutions or small ones—must know where to seek advice, when to take it, and when to disregard it. In turn, they must give evidence of good judgment so that their own staffs may turn to them with confidence for the guidance needed in accomplishing their own jobs.

Initiative, according to Webster, is "self-reliant enterprise." This is a good quality to develop for anyone hoping to take an upward rather than a level path in the profession. Libraries need leaders who can find new methods and areas of service and new ways to put the old ones to better use. A "pint of initiative" mixed with a "pint of judgment" used often in large doses should produce a healthy library that could not only keep pace with today's world but, at times, be a little ahead of it.

Platforms, television cameras, microphones—these are no strangers to the librarian of today. He must meet many people in the course of a day, singly and in groups. He must know how to put his thoughts into clear, understandable words. He must be able to meet reporters, to persuade legislators, to interest laymen. He must also be able to put his thoughts clearly and forcefully on paper. Always, whether he does it by pen or tongue, he must present the role of libraries graphically and well so that the profession he has chosen will be understood by those about him, and through that understanding advance in its usefulness to mankind.

Imagination and curiosity are qualities every librarian should cultivate. Einstein said "Imagination is more important than knowledge." This applies particularly to the librarian who cannot possibly know everything about every subject his patrons may ask about. Imagination, however, tells him where to look for the right answer. Asked to locate a quotation, for instance, he may turn first to the many collections and dictionaries of famous sayings. Not finding it in these logical sources, his imagination comes to his aid. "It sounds like a family motto," he says to himself and turns to the books on heraldry—and there it is. Curiosity keeps him looking for answers he cannot find at first try; it keeps him investigating new books, new magazines, new pamphlets, so that his store of knowledge grows every day. Like a detective, he must put himself in the other person's place. He must imagine where an answer could be, who might have said something like this, in what situation this event might have occurred.

With all this should go a sense of humor. First, it makes the job more fun. One can enjoy the light and foolish things found in print. One can appreciate without cruelty—rather with a greater pleasure in the variety of human nature—the funny things that happen every day. Like the little boy who asked for a book on how to be President of the United States because that was what he aimed to be. Or the one, not sure of closing time, who asked innocently, "When will the library end?"

True humor springs from a lively intelligence. It enables

the librarian to meet and to weather the vicissitudes of the professional life: the all-too-frequent lack of sufficient funds, books, and equipment; the misconceptions of what a library —and just as important, a librarian—is; and the daily necessity of meeting, pleasing, and working with a variety of people.

Earlier in this chapter a librarian was quoted as saying that an essential qualification for the job is good feet. One of the greatest revelations to students who do field work in a library is the physical energy the job takes. Books are heavy and they must be handled many times a day. There are distances to walk in any library, and they must be walked over and over. There are stairs to be run up and then down to get to workrooms, stacks, or storage space. While the hours in the working day are usually regulated so that the standard eight-hour stint prevails, a librarian frequently works some of these eight hours in the evening. Most public and university libraries are open from morning to nine or ten at night, and six—sometimes seven—days a week. The staff must share the night and the Saturday and Sunday work.

In addition to a healthy body, the prospective librarian should have a healthy mind. Contrary to the general idea that a library is a calm and peaceful haven, it is beset with the pressures and deadlines common to most large businesses. Here that sense of humor plus a true sense of values helps to maintain a balanced outlook.

Special Interests and Talents

Few other professions offer such excellent opportunities for combining talents or hobbies with your daily work.

The man who is interested in science, who has an aptitude for chemistry or physics, let us say, and who combines a major in these fields with his library science will find a good field in the libraries of big industries or in the special departments of a university or large public library.

There are business libraries where training and experience in business and economics are sought. Law libraries and medical libraries need librarians with education in these fields. Indeed, there are law libraries where librarians have law degrees as well as their library degrees.

Interest in teaching, social work, literature, religion—all can be combined profitably with a library career. Such talents as art, music, and writing have double value. You may have an inclination to one of these arts but lack sufficient ability to be an artist, a musician, or an author. You can put your interest and your knowledge to good use helping others in a music, art, or literature department.

On the other hand, if he has the ability to *do* as well as to *appreciate* the librarian will find himself equally able to help others and still further his library work in another way. For instance, the artist will find scope for his talents in producing exhibits, designing book lists, annual reports, and other printed pieces; the author, in writing about the library and his work—not only for newspaper releases, annual reports, and so on, but also for the professional magazines. An actor will find that many platforms open up to the person who can tell stories, who will speak about the library and its work, who can bring to others the romance in books. There are microphones and television cameras, and there are puppet stages waiting for the able performer from the library.

So, if you want to be a librarian, if you are a healthy, well-rounded person who likes books and people; if you want to serve others; if you see the humor in human beings and in words; if you have an active mind that seeks knowledge; if you have all these, you are halfway there, and you should be a good one.

TWO

Your Investment

THERE ARE PEOPLE who seem to know from the cradle exactly what they want to be. They are not tempted by the usual short-lived urges common to most youngsters to be a heroic fireman, a daring parachute jumper, a bareback rider, a spotlighted trapeze artist, a long-lashed movie star or a white-uniformed nurse. They fix their eye on their goal in kindergarten and begin their preparation to attain it.

Most people, however—at least through grade school—dally with the notion of various careers, trying on first one and then another like a suit of clothes. If one can make a decision in high school, he will make better academic preparation for his profession. Certainly by the time he reaches college, a student should have a fairly firm notion of what he wants to be in order to prepare for it suitably and profitably.

Surveying the Field

Anyone considering the field of librarianship should consider the many types of libraries in which he might work. In those many types of libraries are many specialized kinds of work. So—the student must take thought as to what kind of

36

work he wants to do where.

In such a preliminary survey a young man or woman can find help by discussing the kinds of librarianship with his school or public librarian and with his guidance counselor. Materials on the various fields can also be obtained from the American Library Association.

While the profession could be subdivided endlessly, certain broad divisions could be used for this preliminary survey. In round numbers there are approximately 2,000 college and university libraries in this country; 7,500 to 10,000 public library units; 3,000 special libraries including those in hospitals, associations, industry, business, and government; and about 20,000 school libraries. Estimates predict a sharp increase in these figures along with the increase in population.

John Eastlick says in "The Sixties and After," a special report to the Federal Relations Committee of the Library Administration Division of the American Library Association: "It is NOT unrealistic to expect that by 1970 80,000 professionally trained librarians actively engaged in library work will be needed to serve the population of 210,000,000 anticipated by the Bureau of the Census."

These 80,000 librarians will be working in many types of libraries and in all sorts of capacities. In a small library, in addition to administering the operation, the librarian may be personally involved in all of its activities. As a library grows, the work is subdivided and the activities become more and more specialized.

As his acquaintance with libraries and with library methods increases, the candidate will discover that many paths branch from the main road. At the outset, they can be divided broadly into services to readers and technical services. In serving readers a librarian will do reference work, reading guidance, advisory work, and will take part in all the activities involved in the borrowing and use of library materials. Within this framework there are subdivisions such as those made by age—service to children, to young people, to adults. Technical services cover the selection, acquisition, organization, indexing, and processing of library materials as well as other details of library operation and maintenance.

Since library schools offer courses to prepare the student for work in these various fields, and since it is possible to specialize in one of them, the student who defines his interest early will be the one who arranges his course of study to the greatest advantage.

A librarian must be a graduate of an accredited library school. In most instances this means four years of college resulting in a bachelor's degree, and a fifth year or more of study in a library school. There are colleges which offer library courses within the four-year program. These serve as a basis for graduate study; as preparation for part-time jobs as teacher-librarians; and, in some cases, in small libraries, for positions requiring work under supervision. Anyone planning to make librarianship his lifework, however, must have his master's degree if he is to win status or advancement in his field. Indeed, most libraries now require the master's degree as a condition of employment.

Choosing Your Library School

In the early days of the library profession, some libraries operated their own training classes in which staff members were taught skills and techniques. Professional training has come a long way since then as it has in many other fields. Now great stress is laid on broad educational background, acquaintance with many areas of knowledge, and intensive study in as many fields as possible.

Because professional librarianship requires a master's degree, it presupposes a college education. Choice of a college will depend upon family traditions, finances, geographical location, academic standing, personal tastes, and many other factors. The student should, of course, choose an accredited college.

Some library schools require a certain number of undergraduate courses in library science. Others deplore using any of the undergraduate period for preprofessional training, preferring the student to use this time to increase his knowledge in other disciplines. If the library school in which you intend to enroll does require preprofessional courses, it would be wise to elect a college which offers those courses. Otherwise these credits will have to be acquired when you reach the graduate school, proving costly in both money and time.

The same factors which affect your choice of a college may also determine the choice of your library school. Leontine Carroll, assistant professor in the School of Library Service at Atlanta University, found that in choosing their library school, students of that university indicated these as the main influences:

> reputation of the university
> reputation of the library school
> geographical location
> costs

These are not the only factors but they are ones which must always be considered along with any other personal reasons the student may have.

The term "accredited library school" now means a school accredited under the 1951 American Library Association standards published in the ALA *Bulletin* for February 1952, pages 48-49. These apply only to graduate programs completed after a minimum of five years of study beyond high school which normally lead to a master's degree. In 1962 there were thirty-four such schools in the United States and Canada. A student may find an up-to-date list of these schools published annually in the December issue of the ALA *Bulletin*. A copy of the bulletin should be available in his school or public library. A list may also be requested from ALA headquarters in Chicago. Because location influences choice of a school, the list given in the appendix is arranged by states.

Columbia University's School of Library Service, established in 1887, is the oldest library school. Pratt Institute, the second oldest, founded in 1890, claims to be "the oldest library school in continuous existence."

Library schools offering a program leading to a doctoral degree are the University of California, Columbia University, the University of Illinois, the University of Michigan, Rutgers University, the University of Southern California and Western Reserve University.

Many college students rely on summer school either to shorten the years spent on their education or to make it possible for them to work and go to school at the same time. These same needs are common to students in the graduate library schools. All of those on the accredited list in the United States offer their curricula in the summer as well as in the regular academic year. McGill in Montreal does not. The summer session at Toronto is open only to students who are enrolled in the six-year program.

No correspondence courses are given or accepted for credit toward degrees by accredited library schools.

Unaccredited Programs

A student may find that his college or university offers a library program although it does not have an accredited library school. There are some two hundred such programs in the United States, the college or university offering twelve or more semester hours in library science. Many of these are designed to prepare school librarians for certification. Certification requirements are under the jurisdiction of the departments of education in the various states.

Requirements for Admission to an Accredited Library School

The French teacher, seeking to comfort her bewildered class, tells them: "In the French language you have the rule. Then there is the exception to the rule. Then you have the exception to the exception which brings you back to the rule again."

Like the French language, library schools have some common requirements but there are enough exceptions to once again warrant a caution to the prospective student. Check with the school or schools in which you are interested well in advance to ascertain individual requirements.

Some generalizations can be made. The majority of schools require:

1. Graduation from an accredited four-year college or university.
2. A good undergraduate record. This is described in various ways; i.e., "C+ or B," "approximately B," "upper one-half (or one-third) of class," "satisfactory record," and so on. Some require a B average in library school prerequisites or from out-of-state students. No matter what phrases are chosen to describe it, the requirement is unmistakable. A candi-

date for library school must maintain a better than
average scholastic record.

3. A reading knowledge of a foreign language. California and Chicago require two. So do certain
specializations. Proficiency in a language may be
evidenced by examination or by credit—the school
you choose will spell this out.

4. The ability to type is regarded as a valuable asset
to a library school candidate. A few schools require
it; most recommend it.

5. Depending upon the school an interview may be
(1) required (2) requested (3) thought desirable.

Almost every library school and everyone advising a college student who is planning to enter library school will
recommend that he take a strong liberal arts program in
his undergraduate work. Some schools require a certain number of hours in this field, or evidence of a well-rounded
program of undergraduate study. The American Library
Association states in *Professional Education for Librarianship:*

Undergraduate study should introduce various fields of
knowledge and include somewhat intensive study in a subject
field. Considerable knowledge of the physical sciences and
social sciences is important in present-day library service. A
librarian is expected to have background in history and
American and English literature, a reading knowledge of at
least one modern foreign language, usually French, German,
Spanish, or Russian, and some ability in research methods.

Here again you see that if you decide in your undergraduate days the kind of librarian you hope to be you can make
preparation plans. For instance, if you want to get into
scientific or industrial libraries you might major in chemistry.
Anyone interested in art or with some artistic talent might

look for a future in the library of an art museum or the art department of a large public library; he would naturally elect a good many courses in art. Business and economics, sociology, philosophy—all are valuable to the embryo librarian. One who inclines toward cataloging, reference work, bibliography, or toward college, university or other scholarly libraries will want a reading knowledge of at least two modern foreign languages—French and German being preferable.

To quote again, this time from the bulletin of the Graduate School of Library Science, University of Illinois:

> For a career in library work, a sound well-balanced intellectual background is needed. By its nature, the work of the librarian is far-ranging and encyclopedic in subject coverage, even in the most highly specialized libraries. History, literature, the social sciences, the natural sciences, and foreign languages are all valuable to the prospective librarian.
>
> In addition to a broad general education, the student should develop a strong major in some subject area during his last two years of undergraduate work or in graduate study. Such subjects as chemistry, physics, musicology, education, engineering, law, agricultural sciences, art, and history are particularly needed in modern library development and when combined with library training lead to a great variety of interesting well-paid library positions.

Some library schools require an entrance examination. Several require vaccination, medical or physical examinations, or certificates of health and vaccination.

Undergraduate Library Science Prerequisites

It has already been indicated that there is a division of opinion on requirements for undergraduate study in library science. Some schools require none at all. On the other hand one requires as much as eighteen semester hours. Others vary from six to twelve semester hours.

Leon Carnovsky, professor in the Graduate Library School at the University of Chicago, has written: "I should myself prefer that students who plan to enter an accredited library school do not take any undergraduate library science courses at all and devote their full time in college to the traditional areas of the arts and sciences."

Requirements for a Master's Degree from Library School

Just as every school has individual entrance requirements so does each establish its own exit requirements with a degree in hand.

Residence of at least two semesters is asked by almost all, a few schools requiring more. Toronto requires that the course be taken in one academic year. Most schools find that the master's program requires two semesters and a summer session or four quarters.

With very few exceptions the student must maintain a B average.

The majority of schools require a final comprehensive examination. There is much wider latitude in the thesis requirement, however. Atlanta, Catholic University, Kentucky, and North Carolina require a thesis. Texas Woman's University requires one for the M.A. but not for the M.L.S. degree. Emory asks for one for the M.A. and M.S. degree but not for the Master of Librarianship. The University of Minnesota requires one under its Plan A but not for Plan B; Oklahoma asks for one for the degree of M.A. in L.S. but not for M.L.S. When a thesis is not required, a school will often ask for a report as evidence that the student has ability to do research and is trained in research methods.

Some schools require field work in libraries, and each has

certain specific courses that every student must take if he is
to win his degree.

Just what form that degree will take will also vary. From
the list of schools in the appendix, the prospective student
can see that once through library school, he may write one
set of letters after his name while a friend from another
school may boast an entirely different set. The M.A. and
M.S. offered by several schools are familiar; they signify a
master's degree in many subjects. M.A. in L.S. and M.S. in
L.S. designate Master of Arts (or Science) in Library
Science. Master of Library Science is shortened to M.L.S.
Master of Librarianship, shown in the list of library schools
as M.L.'ship is also found as M.L.S. and M. Libr.

Each degree shows that the one who bears it has completed
successfully the course of study entitling him to a master's
degree in the field of librarianship. It has been shown that
the course of study will vary according to the school but all
consist of graduate work leading to a graduate degree.

In Dollars and Cents

Times change and so do dollar values. What is said about
costs today will be contradicted tomorrow. A candidate for
librarianship must count on a bachelor's degree plus one
year in a graduate library school. How much money is
needed to finance that education?

Costs of both college and graduate school will be influ-
enced by several factors. Out-of-state residents attending
a state university pay a higher tuition. It costs more if the
student lives away from home while attending school. However, those who do live at home must remember to count the
costs of transportation and lunches in addition to tuition,
fees, and books. In 1960 Columbia estimated that the annual

cost for the student living at home was about $1,000 less. This figure will depend upon the school and its location.

The American Library Association sets the estimated cost of the two semesters and a summer session or the four quarters needed to win the master's degree at between $1,500 and $3,000.

The necessary college education which precedes the master's degree will likewise come with widely varied price tags. Like clothes and cars, colleges command different rates, depending upon the quality of their product, their exclusiveness, and whether or not they are designed for the luxury trade. In addition, the part of the country in which the college is located will affect the cost. So will the student's own tastes and his situation. Does he live at home? Does he drive a car? Is he married? Does he carry his lunch? Does he combine sports, cultural, and social activities with his classes? A nationwide study made in 1960 set the average cost of a year at college at $1,550.

Other estimates set annual costs at a range from $800 for a student living at home and attending a state-supported school to $3,000 for one attending a private, exclusive institution.

Financing Your Education

Every student with a good scholastic record should investigate the opportunities available to him through scholarships, grants, and similar aids. In the final analysis he should always consult the school which he plans to attend, as scholarships offered by individual institutions are not always publicized at large.

For a preliminary survey, however, he may ask the American Library Association for general background information. Through its division of library education, the association has published a list which gives an idea of the kind of financial help available. These include fellowships, scholarships, grants-in-aid, loan funds, and other assistance for library education.

There are scholarships offered by associations which sometimes are open only to members of that association. Library-connected groups, such as the Friends of the Library, will offer a stated sum toward tuition to members of the library staff. These usually carry the proviso that the recipient work on the staff for a certain length of time after he receives his degree. Schools have scholarships, fellowships, and assistant-ships to offer. Awards are also available in the field of practicing librarianship. These are usually offered in a special field, for instance, an award to a children's librarian for further study in children's literature. Some grants are available only to residents of the city or state in which they are offered.

Because of the long hours of service in a public and university library, it is possible to attend library school and work part time in a library. Indeed, a few hardy souls have worked full time, but this necessarily means that it takes longer to get a degree. Some library schools maintain close relationships with the libraries in the community to help place students who desire work. In other instances, the libraries and the schools have a work-study program by which the library hires the student with the proviso that he will attain his degree in a stated period. His work schedule is arranged to accommodate his scholastic program.

Even when such a formal arrangement does not exist, libraries are usually helpful to aspiring librarians. Clerical and page jobs—which do not require professional education

—are open to students. Library clerks type, file, charge books, register borrowers, and perform similar tasks. Pages and shelvers deliver books to and from the shelves. Supervisors are usually sympathetic in arranging schedules so that the employee can combine class and job.

Many universities and colleges as well as library associations maintain loan funds with very low interest rates. A frequent regulation in such loans calls for no interest while the recipient of the loan is in school and a low rate and small payments after he graduates.

There are schools which offer a deferred tuition privilege. Students who are eligible can, by agreement, pay their tuition in installments. In any event, do not abandon all thought of a library career because you think you are unable to finance an education. Talk over your problems with the college or university. The old truism, "Where there's a will, there's a way," is especially true in regard to education. You may be surprised at the helps available to you if you will inquire.

A Word of Advice

Like all generalized information, the facts in this chapter have been kept very broad in order to cover the widest range of possibilities. For that reason they may not apply in full to any specific situation. They are intended to serve only as guides. Early in your planning you should write to the various accredited library schools in which you are interested—as long as possible before the actual point of enrollment. Study the catalogs. If possible, visit the schools and talk to a faculty adviser. Investigate scholarships, grants, and loan possibilities at these schools.

Consult librarians you know personally—at school or in

the public library. Get their advice on library schools, courses, and aid possibilities.

You are embarking on a career and you wish to make the best possible preparation. It will be an expensive journey, worth the money to be sure, but the traveler should be watchful that his money is spent wisely to bring him the best return for it. You will find that librarians who have already made the trip will be willing and helpful guides.

THREE

Your Education

AMERICANS ARE PRONE to distill the essence of their ideas into catch words or phrases which when used repeatedly become trite and lose the fresh force of their meaning. Yet when we bring them back into sharp focus they make their point very effectively. Two such catch phrases we are today overusing in respect to education at all levels, but they describe so precisely what it is that we must strive for in professional as well as general education that I must ask you to bear with me while I use them tonight.

"Tonight" was April 22, 1960.

The place was the dinner session of a conference on library education held at the Kansas State Teachers College in Emporia.

The speaker was Florinell F. Morton, director of the Library School at the Louisiana State University. She continued:

They are "quality education" and "pursuit of excellence." At a time when we are stressing quality education from the kindergarten to and through graduate education, can we afford to provide less than quality education in our professional programs? If school and college libraries are to support adequately quality programs and if our public libraries are to serve effectively America's pursuit of excellence then the librarians who man these libraries must be prepared to give quality service.

To prepare yourself to give quality service in the type of library you have chosen is the reason you go to library school. It is the reason you spend four years in college and then at least one year in a graduate school.

Your College Life

What to wear in college, to join or not to join a sorority or fraternity, current campus fads—all these are covered by a variety of publications. Fall issues of magazines are devoted to such subjects. College publications are helpful. Pamphlets and books in your library have information for you.

This book deals with your college education only as it is related to your professional goal.

By this time you are probably weary of hearing that a broad education is essential to a librarian. But it is true. As a librarian, nothing that you see, you read, you learn, or you hear goes unused. You notice a picture in a magazine or a small item in the morning paper; you hear a short announcement on the radio or learn a new word; chances are that before the day is out this bit of information will help you answer a patron's question.

In the same way, the knowledge that you amass in your formal education gives you the background and orientation that you need to relate people and subjects, facts and knowledge, books and readers. Your college education will give you an introduction to many fields of knowledge. A wide acquaintance with literature, history, sociology, psychology, philosophy, economics—all these will stand you in good stead. Your four undergraduate years are the time to acquire the proficiency in foreign languages required for entrance into library school, and which you will need to be a good librarian.

While you are gathering to yourself this broad background in college, you should also be looking ahead to the field in which you hope to specialize. If you want to be a children's librarian you will take courses in child psychology; aspiring school librarians should build up the necessary credits in education. If you hope for a career in an art or a music library, plan your college courses to include these subjects. If you are aiming toward administrative jobs, look for courses in public administration, business, management, and the like.

In other words, remember that your graduate work will be concentrated for the most part on library science. Your undergraduate days should be spent in making you a cultured and a cultivated human being, and in acquiring the special subject knowledge that will make you proficient in a particular field of the library world.

How to Study

One important ability must be acquired in college—the ability to study. You have already learned that library schools list a superior scholastic average as an entrance requirement. They also require, with almost no exceptions, a B average for the master's degree. Remember, too, that the farther you progress in higher education the harder you will have to work to maintain that average. You are in a more selected group, with the competition stiffer and the standards higher. To attain a B average in a selected group of 15 to 30 is more of an achievement than to attain one in a class of 150.

Extracurricular Activities

Your doctor will tell you that you must take care of your body as well as your mind. Psychologists will tell you that you need relaxation and social activity. Your common sense should also tell you that part of your education is learning to know people as well as books.

College should be a time for you to indulge in sports— even if only as a spectator—in campus organizations, in social activities. Aside from the reasons of health, both physical and mental, there are selfish professional motives. It has been mentioned that nothing you do goes unused in the library field. If you have made the winning touchdown or only cheered the player who did; if you have swung a tennis racket or a golf club; if you have breasted the tape in a track meet or cheered the winner; if you have sped over the ice in a hockey game or shouted yourself hoarse in the stands; if you have swum in the most elementary fashion or tried the trampoline, you will be better able in a later day to serve the sports enthusiast who comes to your library desk.

Campus organizations give you experience in handling groups, in parliamentary procedure, in planning programs, in dealing with people, and in group persuasion—all of which will be valuable to you later as a librarian. If you have served as an officer of the all-college council, you will have more confidence when for the first time you face your library board or the city council. If you have spoken before your fellow students and the faculty, you will be a more competent speaker before women's clubs, luncheon clubs, service clubs— all the organizations a librarian talks to in his day-to-day life.

If you have been treasurer of a campus club or handled

the finances of a university theater or student prom, you will know the rudiments of handling money, keeping accounts, and making financial reports, knowledge which will stand you in good stead in your library position.

Working on the college paper, the yearbook, or in a creative writing group will help make you a better person to present the library and its activities to community news media, help you write better reports, make you more forceful in drafting staff directives, letters, even memoranda.

Experience in the campus theater will make you a better storyteller as a children's librarian, a better book reviewer. It will give you poise for appearances on the library platform.

And so it goes. Any extracurricular experience you gain in college you will put to good use in a library position.

Cultural Opportunities

Both on and off-campus college students are exposed to cultural advantages which can add to their professional preparation. Authors, political leaders, economists, experts in almost every field appear at convocations, commencement, and at special lectures. Art exhibits, film festivals, and concerts are offered. Students at a college or university which is located in a larger community will find off-campus attractions in art galleries, symphonies, opera, theater. In many cases, special rates are given to students. Museums and art galleries—if they charge admission—usually have certain days set aside when admission is free. The wise student will take advantage of as many of these opportunities as he can, knowing that they make him a more understanding and a more cultivated person, a more interesting individual to know, and, in time, a better librarian.

Friends

In college you should build some of the friendships that last a lifetime with people who feel as you do about fundamentals, who challenge the best in you, who understand you. Some may be fellow students; some may be professors. You will find friends in the graduate school also. There you will make the acquaintance of classmates who will be among the future leaders of your profession. All giants in any profession were once students. You may be one of tomorrow's leaders yourself. So may the pretty girl who sits in front of you; so may the long lanky fellow at the desk behind you.

Preprofessional Training

In Chapter Two it was pointed out that there is a difference of opinion regarding undergraduate library courses.

Among the schools requiring undergraduate credits are Texas Woman's University, Drexel, Emory, Florida, Illinois, Kentucky, Minnesota, North Carolina, Oklahoma, Southern California, Texas, Western Michigan, and Wisconsin. Louisiana asks for an elementary knowledge of library science. Western Reserve requires "a basic general familiarity with the use of libraries and library materials. This requirement may be met either by experience or previous training."

If the school you choose demands preprofessional credits, you will find that your graduate year will combine your library courses with others in subject fields. If not, you will spend the year in library science classes almost exclusively. If you have two bachelor's degrees, one in library science, your graduate school requirements—even the number of credits you will need—will differ. Find out early in your planning what your school requires in preprofessional credits so that you will be all set to go when you reach the graduate level.

Schools requiring undergraduate courses are likely to include an elementary course in cataloging and classification, the selection of library materials, and an introduction to reference sources and bibliography. The student may also have a foretaste of library administration and philosophy as well as the literature of various subject fields.

Putting professional aspirations aside for the moment, some of these undergraduate courses will be helpful to you in all of your studies. For instance, a knowledge of classification and cataloging, of reference sources and of bibliography, show you the wealth of material available in a library, and how to locate it quickly and easily and put it to your own use.

Suppose you have had these undergraduate courses. When you open the doors of the graduate school you will know the rudiments of library methods, philosophy, and literature. On the other hand, too much time spent in preprofessional subjects may limit your general educational background. If a candidate's training is too heavily loaded with vocational subjects, he may be required to take additional liberal arts courses before he is admitted to full graduate standing.

Slaving over his books at a desk, wrestling with some problem posed by an instructor, the student often longs for some library experience to point up the reason and the need for the course he is taking. Experience translates theory into practice. Some library schools recognize this, and in their catalogs and counseling suggest the desirability of previous training and experience. There are many ways of acquiring this. Bitten by the library bug early in life, some young people volunteer their services to their local library after school and during summer vacation. In high school there are library clubs whose members work as volunteer assistants. Work opportunities in college sometimes include the library. In addition, there are nonprofessional jobs available in public and university libraries—shelvers, pages, clerks, aids. In some places these jobs require a civil service examination or rating. All of them offer a behind-the-scenes view of library work.

The Graduate Curriculum

Finally comes the day when you have your college diploma, that bachelor's degree after your name, your prerequisites and experience in hand, and you are ready for library school.

Graduates who have preceded you will speak feelingly of how hard they studied to get their library degree. According to Rachel K. Schenk, in her article, "The Dread and the Terror," published in the *Journal of Education for Librarianship* in the fall of 1960, things were even worse many years ago. On May 3, 1910, students at Wisconsin signed the following petition:

We, the undersigned members of the class of 1910 request your attention to the following statement of facts and conditions.

On Thursday, April 28, A.M., the schedule contained four lectures, from 8:30 to 12:20. In the afternoon, apprentice work 2:30 to 5:30 and a compulsory lecture from 8:00 to 9:45 P.M.

On that day new work was outlined as follows:

      Reference. Miss Hazeltine, 11 questions.
      Reference. Miss Imhoff, Public documents,
        10 questions.
      Administration. Miss Drake, Preparation
        of a schedule.

Administration. Mr. Dudgeon, Preparation
of a budget.

At the same time, the class is required to be working 3 hours
each day on bibliographies.

Besides this, in each week, it is required that the class examine
15 children's books, and spend three hours in apprentice work in
the Madison Free Library.

On Friday, April 29, the schedule contained lectures 8:30-
10:20 A.M. and 2:30-3:30 P.M. Then the hanging and refresh-
ments committees were kept busy until six o'clock.

. . . In view of the schedule outlined for this week which includes two afternoons of cataloging and one afternoon apprentice work, the class respectfully asks what time is there for
three hours' daily work on bibliographies, together with daily
required work in reference, administration, children's work, and
public documents.

As there are by the calendar 38 working days, 3 of which be-
long to the class for a trip or vacation, until June 14th, the
beginning of examinations, to fill the required 115 hours on
the bibliographies, it is necessary to do more than the required
3 hours of work each day. If the 3 hours are not done each of
the 6 days in the week, it necessitates 6 hours' work the next
day.

In order to do satisfactory work, through the enervating
spring weather, we request that the course in reference, outside
the lecture hour, be discontinued for the rest of the term, or
the work in bibliographies be cut in half.

Since "the hanging committee" has an ominous sound, it
should be explained that it and the refreshment committee
were responsible for the decorations and food for the May
reception held every year.

Present-day students who, like their forebears of a half
century ago, quail at the slavery implied in such a schedule,
can take heart from the enthusiasm of a student enrolled
today at the Graduate School of Library Science at Illinois.

This student, who has had library experience, writes glowingly of "her day":

Within the relatively small student body are students who come from many countries and have had many different types of experiences in different kinds of libraries. This adds to the class discussions and to our "out-of-class" learning. The faculty members encourage an objective critical approach, and yet they are so intimately involved in library activities throughout the country (and, indeed, the world) that our studies have a solid background of information drawn from the actual library field. The library school library is an exciting place for anyone who has struggled with on-the-job library problems because so many answers and provocative ideas can be found there. The staff of the university library treat the students almost as if they also were staff members (as many of those who work part time are) and include them in their activities. And, of course, beyond the library school is the university with all of its stimulating people, concerts, lectures, etc. So, in a typical day, a student would attend one or two lectures, read, think, talk, and enjoy whatever recreation he chose—from recorder playing to swimming.

Basic Courses

Having studied their catalogs you will already know that the names of the courses vary from school to school.

Courses will vary from year to year as well. What you take today will not be the same as what a student will take five years from now. It will differ even more from courses offered twenty, thirty, fifty, a hundred years hence. Education keeps pace with the world it fits human beings to live in.

No matter how their titles differ in the catalogs, there are certain courses which every student will usually take before he leaves library school with his master's degree. You will recognize a few as the same as the prerequisites demanded for enrollment in some schools.

One is a course in cataloging and classification in which you are taught how to organize library materials for use. You learn how to classify books and other materials into their proper subject areas so they will be grouped with related works, readily accessible. For instance, should a book on physical geography be placed with other books on geography or with geology? Is this particular study of Shakespeare more of a biography or a work of literary criticism? You will learn how to catalog them so that other staff members, as well as the library's patrons, can find them. Catalogers, you discover, forge the key to the library's collection. In this course you will also learn how to establish and maintain the files which are the permanent record of the library's holdings —records which are turned to for insurance purposes, for inventory, for evaluation and similar needs. Most schools combine laboratory sessions with these classes. In them the student puts to work the theory learned in classification and cataloging lectures. He actually classifies and catalogs books. Library schools have special collections for this purpose in which you will meet almost every kind of problem which has ever puzzled a cataloger.

You will take a course in reference service. You cannot be around librarians long without hearing a lot of talk about "tools." When a librarian uses a "tool" he doesn't pick up a hammer, a wrench, a shovel, or a pick; instead, he will reach for a catalog, an index, a bibliography, a concordance, a compendium—in other words, a book. In the reference course, no matter what it is called, you will be introduced to such tools. You will learn about library materials and how to use them to answer the questions your patrons bring to you.

Another course you will take which is offered under a variety of names is one that introduces you to the administration of all kinds of libraries; the systems and methods used in the business end of a library—financial records, circulation of materials, registration of borrowers, and other procedures common to all libraries; the theory of library service and its philosophy. In some schools this will also give you a taste of library history.

Do you know that picking out the books and other materials for a library is one of the librarian's most important jobs? Book selection is a basic course—seldom called by those two words—which will give you the principles of selection and evaluation. You are introduced to the various publications which aid the librarian in the selection process such as reviews, bibliographies, and lists and are taught how to evaluate them, too. Librarians must know the most important books, authors, and even publishers in given subject fields. Your first selection course will be an overview. Later courses will be more detailed as you take up the literature of various subjects.

In selection, a librarian considers more than the buying of fine books. He must also consider which books best fit the needs of the users of his particular library. He must buy for present needs and he must buy for future needs. He must try to "balance" the collection.

If you think of bibliography as the list of books you consulted in writing a term paper you may wonder why you will be required to take a graduate course in it. In fact, in library school you will take many courses dealing with bibliography as "the history or description of books and manuscripts, with notices of the editions, the dates of printing, etc." as Merriam Webster defines the term. At first you will be introduced to national and trade bibliographies, terms which mean the listings of books published in various nations and in various periods, lists put out to aid printers, publishers, and book dealers over the centuries. In electives (the courses you select for yourself) you will be given the opportunity to study bibliography in its second sense as defined by Webster: "A list of writings relating to a given subject or author."

Bibliography of the Humanities, Bibliography of the Social Sciences, Bibliography of the Sciences—these are three courses which almost every school lists among its required courses although some few list them as electives. Some schools require two of the three. Usually the requirement hinges on the student's specialization. These courses deal with the scope of the literature in the given field. They give the student a comprehensive survey of the outstanding names and trends in the field, the classic as well as the current titles of its literature so that the prospective librarian has the essential knowledge necessary for basic book selection, reading guidance, and reference work in each field.

Finally, you will probably be required to take a course that deals with research, a course which will be most important to you. This will teach you the principles of scientific thinking, how to distinguish valid and reliable evidence, and how to analyze and interpret data. You will make the acquaintance of such techniques as the normative survey, experimental study, causal-relationship analysis. Here, too, you learn the essential guides to research literature and how to prepare a research report.

Elective Courses

"The required courses," says Pratt Institute's 1961 catalog, "present a basic core of information that is common to all librarians."

Elective courses, on the other hand, develop the student's

knowledge in the special fields of interest which he has chosen
for his career. For instance, a required course in administration gives him a basic understanding of administrative principles and problems common to all libraries. In an elective
course he pursues the special problems and principles found
in the kind of library he hopes to administer—public library
administration, school library administration, or college and
university library administration.

In addressing the prospective student, Western Reserve
says it this way:

Special programs of electives are designed for students who
wish to prepare for service to children or young adults in public
or school libraries. For students who prefer work with adults it
is possible to choose electives which concentrate in various
areas, for example, public library service, reference, extension,
or technical services, the college, university, special library, or
special subject fields, or documentation.

The Peabody bulletin comments:

. . . Unusual opportunities for specialization are afforded not
only to those who intend to concentrate on university, college,
school, and public librarianship but also for those interested in
the special fields of music librarianship, medical librarianship,
religious librarianship and . . . regional librarianship.

Such statements emphasize the many reminders given in
this book that you should have made some decision as to the
type of library work you wish to do before planning your
program. Unless you decided what you wanted to be when
you exchanged booties for shoes, you will want some help
in making your decision.

What are some of the helps you should look for?

YOUR IMPRESSIONS: Don't trust these too much if they are

not based on knowledge. Students coming from a small community with a drab, undernourished public library sometimes think all public libraries are the same. They are dazzled by the huge resources, the impressive buildings of the large university they attend and again, working from a single instance, they generalize about college libraries. Or a high school librarian may have been severe with you when you talked in the library way back in your sophomore year, and ever since you have ascribed to all school librarians that sharp voice which you remember so well and which—you forget—you deserved. You know from plays and books that newspapers, hospitals, and advertising are romantic and glamorous so you conclude that special libraries in newspapers or hospitals or advertising agencies must be romantic and glamorous. What may not have shown up in those plays and books is the hard work and the necessary routine which mark each day in any line of work—from schoolroom to operating room, from library to reporter's desk, from study hall to the account executive's new campaign. So, investigate all library fields; don't trust your own opinion based on emotion.

KNOWLEDGE: How can you get this in advance, so to speak? First, you can get it through work. Try one of those part-time, or summer, nonprofessional jobs that have been described in preceding pages. Talk to many kinds of librarians about their work. Visit libraries—many of them. Read articles and books about libraries of all kinds.

COUNSEL: Ask your librarian for advice. You will also have an adviser or a counselor in college. Seek his guidance. Your library school counselors have valuable help for you. They will see in you capabilities, talents, attributes which fit you especially well for a certain field or fields.

Your decision on specialization may well affect your choice of library school. The number of courses vary, depending upon the size of the institution. The excellence of specific courses is naturally different in different schools. "Naturally" because the abilities of instructors vary, and the resources of a particular course will often depend on the area in which the school is located. For instance, a library school in a large metropolitan area would offer its students more opportunity to observe and to visit special libraries. Another consideration for students in some lines is the opportunity to pursue specializations in other schools in the university, combining these with his library courses.

By this time you may be impatient to know just what elective courses will be available to you. All courses vary in title and to some degree in content. The names and descriptions given here are generalized. Remember, not all of these are offered in every school.

Most offer a course in public library administration. It may be called just that, or it may be called public library service, public and regional library administration, municipal and county library administration, problems in public library administration, American public library, public libraries, county and regional library service, or larger units of library organization. Some of these names indicate variations in emphasis, and the student may take more than one. These courses take up the problems of administering tax-supported institutions: their government, objectives, and function; finances and control; personnel; organization, extension, and program of services; buildings and equipment; measurement and evaluation of program; cooperation with schools, special groups, and activities in the community; the library's responsibilities.

But suppose you have not cast your lot with public libraries?

Another course you will find at most schools is one on the administration of college and university libraries called something like this: college and university library administration, library administration in higher education, college and university libraries, university library administration, junior college library administration. Like those in the public library field, such a course introduces you to the job of running a library. You will learn about organization, equipment, buildings, budgets, personnel, public relations, and the like, with special reference to this type of library. There would be, in addition, consideration of the functions of research, service to the scholar, the library's relationship to the curriculum and its service to the students, to the faculty, and to the academic administration—all of which must be special concerns of the head librarian of a college or university.

Then there is school library administration. These courses relate the problems of function, administration, organization, and services to the school. The prospective school librarian must learn about the planning and equipment of this type of library; the relationship to the teachers, principal and school administration; to theories of education, and to the curriculum.

As you go through the library school catalogs you will also find courses in special libraries as a general class. In some schools you will find further courses particularizing special libraries—in technical libraries, medical libraries, law libraries, music libraries, religious libraries, and so on—to prepare you to be a more effective specialist.

Closely related courses for the future library administrator are found in schools offering a large curriculum. These might include personnel administration, personnel relationships, or human relations in library administration, to name some examples. There are other courses which will take your administrative ambitions even further; i.e., school library supervision would prepare you for the organization and administration of a whole system of school libraries rather than just one.

Suppose you plan to be a children's librarian. Then you will look for a course in children's literature which will teach you the history as well as the best in modern contemporary writing and illustration of books for children. It will teach you how to select and build a balanced collection. You will be interested in courses in storytelling which will guide you in selecting, adapting, and presenting stories to youngsters of various ages. In some schools you will find special courses in the organization and administration of library services to children.

The candidate who inclines more toward work with the adolescent or teen-ager will find similar courses stressing selection of materials for young people and the guidance of their reading.

Just as there are courses in working with the child and the young adult, so are there courses for librarians wishing to specialize in work with adults. You will find general courses in the reading process which relate to all ages. You will find others dealing with educational and advisory services. There will be such courses as The Library and the Adult Reader, Reading Guidance for Adults, Studies in Reading, Library Service and Materials for the Adult, Reading and Reading Interests, Reading Improvement in Libraries. These deal for the most part with adult education, selection of materials for adults, reading guidance, and reading improvement programs.

Librarian's Reading is a course found in some catalogs which may puzzle you at first. It is not an inquiry into what you read or what other librarians read. Rather, it is a survey of landmark books, contemporary authors, critics, editors, and translators—in reality, one of the courses which will aid you in book selection. In other schools the same material is taught under different names.

You will discover courses dealing with special types of materials. A course in government publications will teach you their nature and use as well as how to select, acquire, and process the publications of municipal, state, and our own federal government, those of foreign nations and of the United Nations.

Another special field which is steadily receiving greater emphasis is that of audio-visual aids. Courses in this cover the problems of selecting and using the materials and equipment, of training personnel, and of organizing these complex types of materials for use. The list of these grows daily; it once dealt mainly with recordings and films. Now courses cover these plus slides, filmstrips, microfilms, microcards, transcriptions, graphic materials, radio and television. Other examples of specialization offered by some schools but not by others are courses in maps and cartobibliographical aids, in periodicals and serials.

Remember those required courses in cataloging and classification? You can choose advanced courses in these as well, along with some in technical processes. These will take up the history of the subject, comparative processes, contemporary problems, research in the field, and new developments.

Advanced work in reference materials and methods is sometimes offered under a title as explicit as that. Other schools name the courses differently, and such methods and materials may be found in subject fields.

Almost every library school offers the student an opportunity to study the history of libraries, of books, and of printing. Sometimes these are combined in a survey course; in other instances, more detailed courses give a wider and more scholarly background. These courses appear under such titles as History of Books and Libraries, History of Libraries (which can be subdivided into History of Ancient and Medieval Libraries, History of Scholarly Libraries, and History of Popular Libraries). Such titles are more or less self-explanatory and most courses take the student from the libraries of Nineveh to the modern tax-supported public library of the present day.

Courses in the history of printing may appear under such labels as Modern Book Production, Making of the Book, History of the Book, History of Books and Printing, or Development of the Book. There are courses which are devoted to just one phase of the book's history, such as medieval manuscripts. These teach the student the origin and evolution of the alphabet and of scripts; the invention and spread of printing; relationship between books and the social conditions of the periods in which they were produced; and appreciation and understanding of the book arts. A knowledge of libraries, books, and print, with which the student will later spend his professional career, seem indispensable to making him a well-rounded librarian. For this reason a historical course is required in some schools.

Courses dealing with the library's role in society are rather generally found. Those called by such titles as Library in

Society are designed to orient the student in a general over-view. They treat of the development and function of the library as a social institution, the various kinds of libraries, their organization, operation, standards, cooperation and trends as well as the opportunities, responsibilities and professional status of librarians. On the other hand, such courses as Public Communication and the Library, Communication Roles and Responsibilities of Libraries, The Library and Mass Media of Communication, and Content Analysis all consider the library as an agent of communication, dealing with the effect and use of mass media, propaganda and censorship, responsibilities, regulations, and community relationships.

When you are going over the courses of study you will probably find something like this: Directed Study, Directed Research, Special Study, Studies in Librarianship, Independent Study. You will also find some courses related to writing and preparing for a thesis. As you know, not all schools require one. Usually a thesis can be written in place of taking a certain number of formal credits in class. Even though they may not ask for a thesis, most schools require some evidence that a student has mastered the process of doing qualified, scholarly research, demonstrating his ability to assemble, organize, and present it in a clear and acceptable form. To that end they will demand one or more formal papers. In some cases the student registers for Directed Study, Special Study, or the like and pursues independent investigation of a library problem which has been approved by his adviser. This type of study presupposes a knowledge of research methods; hence, the courses offered in research. It also requires self-discipline. Many a student has found that it is harder to be his own taskmaster and to set his own goals and regimen of study than it is to follow one set by an instructor.

You may find field work asked for in your library school. For a student majoring in special libraries, field work is required in such a library; county library specialists do theirs in a county library, etc. Field work is also required occasionally in place of library experience. In any event, field work is valuable in relating the theory learned in the classroom to the practical operation and service of a library.

This discussion here has not been a complete list of every course taught in every library school. It serves only to give the prospective student an idea of the variety and content of library courses, the differences he may find in the curricula offered in the various schools. As those needs change, the preparation required of the librarian who hopes to meet them must also change.

FOUR

Finding Your Job

"GET THY SPINDLE and thy distaff ready, and God will send flax," says the proverb.

Your diploma authorizing you to use that long-sought M.A. after your name shows that you have your spindle and your distaff ready. Where do you look for the flax?

School Placement Service

Almost all library schools have a placement service, whether it is formally labeled so or not. One criterion by which they judge their own performance is the number of students employed. Another is where and how well they are employed. No school will guarantee employment of a student. However, during the past several years and certainly for some years yet to come, there will be several jobs for every eligible librarian. Most library schools have more requests for recommendations than they have graduates to recommend.

Your library school advisers will be well aware of your performance as a student and your potential as a librarian. It would be well to see to it that they know what kind of a job you are looking for. You should also pay good heed to their advice as to the kind of position you are best fitted for since usually their knowledge of your ability is more objective than your own. In addition, their acquaintance with libraries is usually wider than yours. They are in a better position to help you decide whether or not a particular job is the most advantageous one for you to accept.

Advertisements

Do not wait until graduation to start looking for that position. If you do, you will find that the best ones will have been plucked from the tree by your farsighted classmates long before the organ sounds the first notes of the commencement processional. Watch the columns of the *Library Journal*, the ALA *Bulletin*, the *Wilson Library Bulletin*, *Special Libraries*, and similar professional publications for opportunities that appeal to you while you are still in your student status. You might also register for civil service examinations.

Recruitment Programs

There are libraries which send recruiting officers to certain library schools to interview students in advance of graduation. You must, of course, be governed by the procedure in your particular situation, but if you have an interest in the library represented and you have the qualifications for the positions they offer, ask for an interview. If nothing else, you will gain valuable experience about the job interview and how to conduct yourself.

Conferences

The American Library Association has a placement service at its annual conference, held in early summer in one or another of our large cities. While most students will not feel financially able to make a long journey without some definite interview in mind, there will be times when some will find the conference is close enough to their home or their school to make the trip feasible.

Attendance at library meetings, local, state, regional, and national, increases your acquaintance among librarians. What is more important, they get to know you. When a vacancy occurs and your application comes in, you are not an unknown quantity.

Letters and Interviews

Do not overlook nearby libraries. Make application to them. It is good experience to be interviewed for a position. When applying in person, make an appointment in advance. It is not in your favor to turn up at the personnel officer's door just as he is trying to write an important report, leaving for a meeting, or struggling with the salary budget. An appointment made in advance assures you of a cordial welcome, and also the time and attention from the interviewing officer which will make the session profitable to you.

Write letters of application to libraries in which you are interested. Keep in mind that these letters represent you with nothing more to plead your cause than a piece of paper and the words on it. First make the letter attractive physically. Use good paper. Type it carefully with wide margins and no erasures. Make it accurate; spelling and grammar should be above reproach. Then be sure that it is clear. Set forth your background, talents, and abilities briefly, modestly, and in a straightforward manner. A librarian should never lack for help when writing a good letter of application. The library is full of books offering advice on the subject.

FIVE

Returns on Your Investment

ENJOYMENT OF LIBRARIES, enjoyment of
books, enjoyment of library work—these are the three most
common reasons for choosing librarianship as a career according to a study made for the Public Library Inquiry of
the Social Research Council. About two-fifths of the librarians surveyed hoped to win financial security and 15 per
cent hoped that a library career would give them a satisfying
position in their community.

In this same study, more than half of the librarians found
that their careers were more satisfying than they expected.
Approximately one-third found what they expected. (Only
2 per cent were very disappointed; 12 per cent were somewhat disappointed.)

From this it would seem that, by and large, if you like
libraries, books, and library work, and choose librarianship as a profession, you should find satisfaction in your
career.

Libraries themselves have a fascination for many people.
This fascination has no relationship to the size of the library,
its physical beauty, or its age. The idea of being surrounded
by books promising future knowledge, escape, excitement—

this appeals even to the nonreader. To the reader it is irresistible.

One who chooses librarianship as a career should enjoy books. His life will be spent among them and with others who enjoy them. It may be a shock at the outset to be told that librarians do not spend their working day reading books. Most of their own personal pursuit and enjoyment of the content of books comes after hours. Then why does someone who enjoys books find satisfaction in a library career? It's because his working day is spent in handling books, finding in them the exact information someone needs, using his own knowledge of books to help another. A librarian lives in a world of books which means that his day is spent with people who know and love them. He has an ear to the publishing world and knows what is being written about and by whom. He sees new books and new editions as they are added to the collection. In some libraries he sees old books, first editions, treasures; he knows the pleasure of handling the very book that might have been read by a great man centuries ago.

For the librarian who seeks to know and understand people, who wants to use his life to help others, there is a reward beyond the grateful "Thank you, I didn't dream the library would answer this kind of a question!" that comes when he turns up a needed fact. His memory is furnished with satisfactions.

You remember the pale woman who confides that since her husband died she has had no interest in life and has finally come to the library to see if perhaps a book may comfort her. There comes the gratification of sending her home with some hopeful titles under her arm, of watching her eyes brighten and her smile appear in the weeks to come as she begins to find new interests in the books you choose for her.

There is the vicarious pride in the successful business built by a baker and his wife who have pioneered in the frozen food business, finding information on freezing methods, packaging, names and marketing—all in the library.

There is the almost parental gratification in watching the serious little boy who in fifth grade asked you for books on "physics, *nuclear* physics!" graduate to the adult department; in reading eventually of his important research work for the government.

No librarian can go home at night without having helped someone in a day, without having earned someone's gratitude.

Prestige

During the early postwar years when housing was hard to find, a member of the staff of a large public library went apartment hunting. After a weary search she found one. Satisfying the landlord on this seller's market was the next hurdle. Landlords and landladies required "references." She turned to the owner and began to give the names and addresses of friends who would vouch for her character and responsibility. In the course of exchanging this information, she mentioned that she worked at the library.

"The library!" exclaimed the landlord. "You work at the library? You don't need any references. The apartment is yours."

Periodically, individual librarians become concerned with their public "image" and pepper the professional press with either indignant or apologetic papers complaining of the lack of understanding of librarianship. True, the librarian found in comic strips, in newspaper jokes, and in radio and television sketches is likely to be a drab, shirtwaisted female who grimly demands silence while she collects fines.

The actual work of most professions is misunderstood. The career Army man winces no doubt at the hardboiled sergeants, the callow second lieutenants, the unscrupulous commanding officers who parade through fiction. Nurses do a great deal more than lean over the beds of wealthy patients, soothing hand pressed to a fevered brow. Actors and actresses spend long, heartbreaking hours preparing for that short, exciting footlighted performance the audience cheers. Stereotypes are convenient symbols and have little regard for individual differences. The drab, shirtwaisted librarian is about as realistic today as the quick-talking reporter with hat on the back of his head and bottle in hand; or the banker who leaves work at noon for the golf course; or the detective who cannot see a corpse in the middle of the living room rug without the help of a brilliant private eye. Yes, every profession has its doubtful image. There may be some drab, shirtwaisted librarians, some bankers who figure a score card quicker than the interest on a mortgage, some detectives who miss the obvious—but to label all their fellows with the same brand shows a shallow disregard of the precious differences in character, mentality, ability, physical makeup, and disposition that make us all individuals and the world an interesting place to be.

A little common sense, a dash of objectivity, a good look at your own impressions and reactions show you that the stereotype a person laughs at in a joke, a cartoon or a sketch is just that—and he does not transfer the image to his friend or neighbor in the profession that is so lampooned. The average man does not think of the librarians he meets and knows as the grim-faced dragons of the comic strip. He thinks of them rather as people he likes. Librarians are usually re-

spected in the community. The chief librarian is invited to
join the important clubs, to serve on civic committees, to
represent the literary, cultural, or educational aspects of a
program. A librarian is respected as one who reads books,
who has had an advanced education, who has a rich cultural
background. Librarians are considered responsible and re-
spectable, and, while most citizens do not think of them as
wealthy, they are credited as "solid" citizens and good risks.
More than that, they have a valued reputation for helpful-
ness and for interest in others.

Jan Struther, author of *Mrs. Miniver*, says it in this
passage from *A Pocketful of Pebbles:*

I have often wondered what it is that makes librarians such
congenial and sympathetic company. I think it is partly because
librarianship is one of the few callings in the world for which it
is still possible to feel unqualified admiration and respect. Almost every other profession has been more or less debunked,
either by sceptical theorists or by the merciless cold daylight of
human events . . . the librarian nowadays is a person of more
than ordinary value and significance. We have always liked him
and respected him, looking upon him as a quiet, helpful member
of society, not very exciting, perhaps, not very heroic, probably
more than a little short-sighted, living in a dim, pleasant world
that smelt faintly of dust and printer's ink and old leather—a
world that seemed to us far removed from what we used to call
the realities of life. But nowadays he is something much more
than that. Or rather, he is what he always was. It is we others
who have changed. We have revised in the last few years our
whole conception of reality. . . . We have learnt at last, in a
painful and difficult school, that the only lasting reality is
thought. The accumulated thought of ages is contained in
books. Books are contained in libraries. So it becomes clear that
the librarian, far from being remote from reality, is living at
the very headquarters of it. He is the guardian of its citadel.

Salaries

One library school professor, known for her unpredictability, startled her class by demanding: "Why did you decide to become a librarian?" After the hapless girl who first got the question had floundered through a hastily mustered reason, the teacher proceeded around the entire class with the same question. The reasons were altruistic for the most part: a desire to serve mankind, an urge to further the search for truth, a love of books. Finally, one forthright student declared: "I have to earn a living and this seemed a good way to do it." And the professor cheered.

Everyone who enters a profession, who spends years and money preparing for it, should expect to be able to earn a living from it. No matter how much he loves books, learning, or his fellowmen, he must be able to keep body and soul together while he inhabits this planet. Most hope to accomplish this with a fair amount of comfort in the bargain.

Although no one enters the library profession to get rich, salaries have shown notable improvements in the last few years. A survey of library school placements made by Donald E. and Ruth B. Strout and reported in the *Library Journal* for June 15, 1962, showed that salaries offered the 1961 graduate in the United States ranged from a low of $2,760 to a fantastic high of $10,200. The *average* salary was higher than ever before—$5,365.

Most recruiting information issued by various libraries, library organizations, or librarians themselves point out that earnings "compare favorably with those in other professions allied with teaching and social service," "have increased appreciably, following closely and in some cases exceeding those paid to teachers, nurses, and social workers," or "compare favorably with those of other professions."

Salaries for school librarians are the same as those of teachers in the same system. Those of special librarians will vary with the organization in which they work.

Because the economy of the time affects all salaries, no blanket statement made in one year can long remain accurate. Salaries change too rapidly. Also, in the library field, salaries vary widely depending upon the size of the library, its use by its public, prevailing rates in the community, and similar factors. However, even library school graduates without experience who are not irrevocably tied to one community or library, but who are free to choose, can be assured of a good beginning salary. How much that salary will rise depends upon a variety of factors in addition to his own ability. There are librarians heading large libraries in the nation's big cities or important libraries in government who command enviable salaries. Librarians in small communities seldom attain really high salaries, but the actual amount of the salary must be judged by others paid in the community and the cost of living there. This cost of living means not only the cost of food, shelter, and clothing, but also the professional cost of living—what is expected of that librarian in the way of memberships, continuing education, professional travel, entertainment, and the like.

Minimum standards for payment of librarians are set forth in *Public Library Service* published by the American Library Association in 1956:

Salaries for staff members should be at a level to attract and hold personnel with the qualifications specified in these standards.

Professional library preparation requires five years of formal education beyond high school, as well as continuing study throughout the practitioner's career in order to keep abreast of new methods and materials. These features alone, aside from the high personality qualifications required, necessitate a high initial salary to attract competent people. In order to hold and reward superior personnel, a substantial range of salary increases through increments and promotions is essential. Since compensation patterns change from time to time, no permanent figures are suggested here.

Rates of pay for professional staff members should be comparable in all grades and stages with rates of pay in other professions with which libraries must compete on a national scale. . . .

As staff members assume specialized duties or greater responsibilities compensation should be correspondingly higher to reflect the higher level of position held.

Able librarians, especially those who develop specialties of one kind or another and who are willing to take on extra assignments, can find many opportunities for making additional money in the library field but outside their daily job. These might include appraisal of old or rare books; classifying and cataloging private or business libraries; acting as a consultant on the location of new library buildings, architectural planning of new buildings, or the organization or service patterns of a library; teaching in a library school or conducting special workshops or seminars; writing and speaking.

With the shortage of librarians in every field and with library schools graduating but a handful each year to meet the demand, it seems that the law of supply and demand can do nothing else but force library salaries upward. Librarianship is not for the man who counts his rewards in annual dividends and gilt-edged certificates, but it does offer a comfortable living on the material side and, on the mental and spiritual side, a luxurious existence.

Hours

Like salaries, library hours vary with the community, the size and type of the library, and the size of the staff. As a general rule, librarians work a five-day week of forty hours or less.

School librarians work the school week with Saturday and Sunday off and no night work, conforming closely to the teachers' schedule, although the library may stay open until a specified hour after the door of the classroom has closed.

Libraries in business and industry conform in a large measure to the hours of the firm they serve.

Public, university, and college librarians should expect some night work. These libraries remain open at night to serve their borrowers. Scheduling is accomplished by staggering the staff. That is, one portion works from opening time in the morning until about the dinner hour. The evening shift comes on around the middle of the day and works until the closing hour which will vary, but is usually nine, sometimes ten, at night. Staff members in public departments share the night work, each one working one or two nights a week. The compensatory morning off appeals to many librarians who find it valuable for shopping, business appointments, and home duties which cannot be handled at night. These libraries also require Saturday and, in some cases, Sunday work. Again, these assignments are rotated with compensatory time off.

Pay for overtime is rarely allowed professional librarians.

Vacations

As does everyone else, a librarian looks forward to vacation and makes good use of it. Vacations for special librarians conform to the pattern of the business or industry they serve and may range from two weeks up. The length of the vacation may depend upon the years of service.

School librarians enjoy the school vacation at Christmas and Easter and in most cases also the long summer vacation of the teacher. Like the teacher, the school librarian is usually paid on a ten-month basis, but the annual amount is as high or higher than that paid to the public librarian for a longer work year.

Vacations for public librarians vary according to the library and the community, but the general pattern is an approximate four-week vacation with pay. Allowances in libraries are described variously: "one month," "twenty-two working days," "twenty-six working days," "four weeks."

ALA's *Public Library Service,* referred to earlier, states that the vacation allowance for professional positions should not be less than one month.

Holiday allowances for school and public librarians are also generous in most cases, the number of holidays being larger than those allowed in business. These might include Washington's Birthday, Lincoln's Birthday, Columbus Day or special regional holidays.

Retirement

Librarians should be covered by pension plans which will guarantee a secure retirement, according to the American Library Association. Most libraries have some type of plan. It may be social security, a state, federal or municipal employees' retirement plan, teachers' retirement program, or the like. A growing number of people favor social security because it allows for more mobility. A librarian who has invested ten, fifteen, twenty years or more in a pension plan is reluctant to give up the benefits and move to another job. Social security credits travel with you. On the other hand, some of the independent plans have greater benefits than social security. Where a private plan exists, employee organizations will usually strive to obtain a compromise plan, combining benefits from both.

Sick Leave and Insurance

Although there is some variation, sick leave is usually 12 days a year, the equivalent of a day a month. Many libraries allow generous cumulative benefits, the employee being able to accumulate up to 90, 100 or 120 days of sick leave.

While many institutions promise group insurance, particularly health plans, there is considerable variation as to who pays the bill. In some cases the employee pays his own premiums. However, the trend is becoming more and more general in both public and private employment for the employer to pay all or part of the cost of hospital and medical insurance.

Because employment conditions, salaries, and fringe benefits are dependent on so many outside factors, a young person considering librarianship as a career should look for the current library situation in the "Librarian Wanted" columns of the *Library Journal*, the *Wilson Library Bulletin*, the ALA *Bulletin* and *Special Libraries*. He will be able to find one or more of these publications in his school or public library. The advertisements will give him a good idea of the going rate in various parts of the country and the fringe benefits available.

Man vs. Woman

Librarianship is popularly considered a woman's profession and certainly the greater percentage of people in the field are women. However, the number of men in library schools has increased sharply. Librarianship is a good field for women and they will feel no discrimination because of their sex at the beginning levels. Many women hold high posts in libraries and earn good salaries.

However, it is a fact recognized by both men and women that men will advance further and at a more rapid pace than women. In other words, men attain higher salaries and top posts at a younger age and with less experience than do their feminine counterparts. City administrators prefer men to head large public libraries. Men usually head large university libraries, also. The trend toward male administrators is a growing one and is a factor in attracting men to the profession.

Women do hold responsible and well-paid positions in libraries, however. They are listened to in professional associations and are important in shaping the goals of librarianship.

Library Associations

Library associations offer many outlets for professional ambitions and satisfaction.

The American Library Association, with headquarters in the heart of Chicago near Lake Michigan (50 East Huron Street, Chicago 11, Illinois), is the national library association, the oldest and the largest national library association in the world. It was founded in 1876 by seven men, all great library leaders—Justin Winsor, C. A. Cutter, Samuel S. Green, James L. Whitney, Fred B. Perkins, Thomas W. Bicknell, and Melvil Dewey. Today its members number over 25,000 and its program extends around the world with

projects in such far-flung places as Ankara, Rangoon,
Tokyo, Munich, Mexico, and Mandalay. The American Library Association, known simply among librarians as ALA,
states as its object: "to extend and improve library service
and librarianship in the United States and throughout the
world. In the furtherance of this objective, it seeks to make
books and ideas vital forces in American life, to make libraries
easily accessible to all people, to improve professional standards of librarianship, and to create and publish professional
literature." This ambitious goal is possible only through the
hard work and dedication not only of a small headquarters
staff but even more of the thousands of members who give
countless hours of volunteer work to extend and improve library service, to make books and ideas vital forces in our
daily lives, to make libraries accessible to all, to enlarge the
body of professional literature.

Such volunteer work is found in all library associations,
state and local, as well as national. Their members are the
ones who gather the bibliographies, make the indexes, write
the guides which when published become invaluable aids to
other librarians and to the public they serve. They are the
ones who appear before Congress and the state legislatures,
before the political platform committees of the major parties
to point out the necessity for books and libraries in a democracy, for legislation to keep ideas free, for funds to bring
books to *all* the people, whether they live on a mountain or
in the valley, not just to the people in cities.

All library associations are looking for workers, librarians
with ideas, talent, and enthusiasm. The American Library
Association has thirteen divisions, five of them called type-of-
library divisions and eight, type-of-activity:

TYPE-OF-LIBRARY

American Association of School Librarians
American Association of State Libraries
Association of College and Research Libraries
Association of Hospital and Institution Libraries
Public Library Association

TYPE-OF-ACTIVITY

Adult Services Division
American Library Trustee Association
Children's Services Division
Library Administration Division
Library Education Division
Reference Services Division
Resources and Technical Services Division
Young Adult Services Division

Each of these is divided into sections and committees. More, acting for the association as a whole, there are special projects, committees, and round tables offering ample opportunity for discussion, for growth, and for the use of an individual's abilities.

State associations offer similar outlets. Most cities of any size have local library clubs. Regional associations made up of several states are found in some parts of the country. Other associations with special interests and with national membership include the American Association of Law Librarians, the American Merchant Marine Library Association, the American Theological Library Association, the Association of American Library Schools, the Association of Research Libraries, the Music Library Association, the Theatre Library Association, the Catholic Library Association, the Educational Film Library Association, the Medical Library Association, the Special Libraries Association, the American

Documentation Institute, the Bibliographical Society of America, and the Council of National Library Associations. Other countries have national associations also. The Canadian Library Association (Association Canadienne des Bibliothèques) is affiliated with the American Library Association and they have held two joint conferences, the most recent one in Montreal in 1960.

Newcomers to librarianship will find a warm welcome in the various library associations. Indeed, if the newcomer has ambition, willingness to work, and fresh ideas, the associations will do more than welcome him. They will offer him opportunities to work. This does more than help the association; on a selfish plane, it helps the young librarian. While the job he is holding as a beginner may seem to be at the bottom of the ladder, the association work gives him an opportunity to demonstrate his leadership, his abilities and talents, his original thinking. Good performance on a committee will call him to the attention of other librarians and will have more to do with bringing promotion and better job offers than will letters of application.

Associations offer other opportunities. An example would be the American Library Association's international program. Librarians are needed for projects in other lands, for exchange visits to other nations as opportunities arise for the exchange of information and the promotion of understanding. International library conferences are also held occasionally.

The People You Meet

Some of the most interesting people in the world use libraries. To be interesting one need not be famous; every librarian has met people over the desk who had fascinating hobbies and ideas yet whose names he never knew. On the other hand, famous people also read books and look for them in the library.

A story is told of a midwestern librarian who looked up from her desk into the eyes of actor Charles Boyer. Behind him stood Charles Laughton. Not unusual when one considers that the two were on tour together in their production of Shaw's *Don Juan in Hell*.

Authors, statesmen, and educational leaders are frequent guests of library associations. Individual libraries bring authors, illustrators, scientists, musicians, actors, poets, and others to their book fairs, seminars, and similar activities.

If a library is distinguished for its collection, its program, or its building, it will be visited by the men and women who come to the city, both from elsewhere in the United States and from other countries. The United States is distinguished for its libraries and its library methods. This is especially true of the public libraries and children's libraries. Tourists from abroad are anxious to see them. They want to know how American libraries operate, how they approach various service problems.

Since World War II government programs have brought foreign librarians to this country to work in American libraries. The opportunity to meet and to work with librarians from India, Sweden, Norway, Egypt, England, the Philippines, Finland, and so on is one which the American librarians find endlessly rewarding. It is a chance to learn foreign ways and manners, customs, and history at first hand. More, such meetings have resulted in lasting friendships, broadening both the heart and mind.

But in librarianship you need not wait for travelers from abroad to make interesting friends. Librarians by nature have a lively mentality and a rich cultural background. Being human, they vary in temperament, ability, personality, and outlook, just like those in any profession. Generally speaking, however, because of their background they appreciate wit, the turn of a phrase, subtle humor as well as the obvious. They travel and have a cosmopolitan outlook. They tend to be liberal in their thinking. They like good food and the number of good cooks in the profession is high. They like the theater and music. Jazz enthusiasts will be found as well as the classical buffs. They do interesting things outside working hours. Running down a list of library friends you will find a man who makes wine, an amateur composer, a Sunday painter, a woodcarver, a metal craftsman, a bird watcher, a concert pianist, a sailing enthusiast. Conversation in a group of librarians will be lively and catholic.

In Place of Paradise

In addressing a library school class, Christopher Morley gave them a quotation from Erasmus: *Assiduus sis in bibliotheca, quae tibi Paradisi loco est.* ("May you be assiduous in your library which is for you a place of Paradise.")

No library recruiter would promise an aspirant to the profession that he would find the profession a Garden of Eden. But you will find many fruits in it. There is no pavement of gold to make you rich, but you can take from the trees a comfortable living, generous fringe benefits, mental growth and enrichment, interesting people, good friends, and endless possibilities for becoming a wiser, better, and more understanding human being.

SIX

The Field: Kinds of Libraries

' "BUT ARE YOU SURE one pilot, alone, can make a flight like that? It's going to be something like forty hours in the air, you know. Say, exactly how far is it between New York and Paris by the route you're going to follow?"

' "It's about 3500 miles. We could get a pretty close check by scaling it off a globe. Do you know where there is one?"

' "There's a globe at the public library. It only takes a few minutes to drive there. I've got to know what the distance is before I can make any accurate calculations. My car's right outside." '

This conversation took place in February 1927 at the Ryan aircraft factory in San Diego. The first speaker was Donald Hall, the company's chief engineer. The other was a tall, lanky young man who was to become a national idol some three months later—Charles A. Lindbergh, the Lone Eagle. They were discussing plans for his plane, The Spirit of St. Louis. He tells the story himself, in his book, *The Spirit of St. Louis* (Scribner, 1953).

At the library, with a piece of white grocery string stretched tight, Lindbergh found that the distance was 3,600 statute miles. Nor was this his only encounter with the public library in those tense preflight days. The young flyer had never done any long-distance flying before, nor had he flown over water. To save weight in his plane he had decided to try his flight over the Atlantic alone, acting as his own navigator. How would he do it? The Navy might be able to help him but he did not care to ask assistance. If he admitted his inexperience, authorities might stop his flight. He scouted the ship chandlers in San Diego and San Pedro for the charts he needed. Then he locked himself in Donald Hall's drafting room to work over them. Finally he had his 3,610 mile route inked in. But so much hung on his success. Dared he risk it on such a simple course? He thought he should seek some kind of check on his own figures. He tells what he did in his own words: "The public library downtown has texts on navigation that give detailed instruction about spherical mathematics. I decide to lay a second route across the ocean by trigonometry."

He learned the procedure. After spending several days on his calculations he felt confident that since the first 1200 miles of the mathematical route coincided so closely with the charted route it would be unnecessary to proceed further. Three months later, on May 20, he landed in Paris, the first pilot to make a solo flight across the Atlantic.

Public Libraries

Many such stories are buried in the shelves of the 8,200 public libraries in the United States. Each person has his own idea of what a public library is. Usually a state, city, county, or regional tax-supported agency is meant when the average man talks of his "public library." It is the proud boast of these libraries that they are truly public, since they exist only when the people themselves establish them. It is the people who seek the legislation and the funds to make a public library a reality. Proud are they also of the fact that the public library, as most Americans know it, is this country's unique contribution to Western civilization.

The place of the library in the city's political structure will depend upon the municipality. Policy matters are usually determined by the library board, a citizen group. The board may be elected or appointed. How they are appointed follows a multiplicity of patterns across the country. The board selects the librarian who administers the library. As a general rule, the board members do not actively participate in the selection of personnel other than the chief librarian, although there are exceptions to this rule especially in small libraries. They act as a public sounding board, playing an active role in public relations. The board is usually concerned with budgets, financial support, buildings, and determination of policy, goals, and program. The staff implements the policies determined by the board.

A public library may be a small one, the only library in the town, and you will be *the* librarian without any professional help. It may be a large system with a network of branches, bookmobile stops, stations, and a many-storied central building, staffed by a crew of professionals, including subject specialists. No matter where it is or what your place in the organization may be, there will always be something interesting going on in a public library.

There was the librarian of a town in Iowa who was chairman of the state library conference to be held in her town. The opening day of the meeting dawned. She drove to the library to find that the firm which had the contract for laying a new roof and which had postponed doing the job for weeks had decided to begin that day. Staggering under this blow she went inside, only to find that the janitor had fallen down the stairs and had been discovered bleeding and unconscious at the bottom. She rushed him to the hospital, returning just in time to meet the conference delegates as they came in, and to murmur hospitably to each: "Won't you come in; please step over the blood."

The library acts as a source of books for the reader and as an information center. Some librarians claim that there is no service which the library cannot becomingly perform. This might be open to some question. Nevertheless, it indicates the active, aggressive attitude that public librarians have developed in taking their place in the community. Along this line of reasoning, libraries have operated radio stations, housed Red Cross classes, supplied community meeting rooms, sponsored concerts and dramatic productions, operated museums and even a planetarium, held art shows, loaned umbrellas on rainy days, and furnished high chairs for the infant offspring of reading mothers.

Talk to any librarian and he will tell you that in his job he does everything. On the other hand, every library job is different. More than that, a good librarian makes his job different because of his own personality. For that reason, although there will be descriptions of some general kinds of library work in this and the next chapter, no attempt can be made to cover all the jobs you can find in the library world. Remember, too, that any description is a general one and will vary with the community, the library, and the individual in the position.

Seventy per cent of the public library systems in the United States (according to the Library Services Branch) serve a population of less than 10,000. Only 3 per cent serve populations over 100,000. This means that many "city" libraries will have a staff and circulation to compare with branches in a large metropolitan system. Although the comparison cannot be followed down to the finest points, some of the similarities between the branch of a large city library and *the* library in a small town are obvious. Each has its own collection to suit the readers of that particular area. The program of exhibits and activities will be planned around the needs and the tastes of that communty. The librarian will represent the library system in that area and will administer that agency. Naturally, a branch library, being part of a larger system, will be less independent than a town library. The money to run the branch will come from the central funds, and the branch librarian will not be responsible for the financing of the system. He will not have to appear before a board of control to plead for his budget. However, a branch librarian will be responsible for the funds which go through his hands and will have to account for them; he will also have to be able to plead his own cause before the library administration if he feels that his branch deserves a larger allotment for books or equipment, more staff, or a better building. Branches vary in size. It would be possible to have a branch with a limited schedule of opening manned by one librarian, though this would be restricted service. Most branches have more than one professional librarian. The staff would include a children's librarian and possibly a young adult specialist, plus clerical and shelving help. Some branches would have much larger staffs.

In large systems there is a growing trend toward the regional branch, a large, busy branch which acts as a center for other smaller branches. The regional branches in turn depend upon the central library. In some cases the bookmobile service will operate from the regional branches.

Let us follow Polly Baker, branch librarian, to work. She arrives early, noting that it must have been busy the night before as desks and tables are still piled with books. Other members of the staff are arriving close on her heels. The telephone rings. Cathy Jensen, one of the clerks, is ill with the flu and cannot make it to work that day. Polly sighs and picks up the schedule. Someone will have to work a "split" day; that is, work through the morning, take the afternoon off, and return in the evening in order to cover Cathy's schedule. She herself will pick up some of the tasks. One is before her. The delivery from the central library was made long before the staff arrived at the branch. She opens the boxes and checks the contents. Here is the historical novel that Mrs. Paddington had asked for. The central library *did* have a copy. Here is a whole package of books and magazines for young Mary McLean who is doing a term paper on new drugs developed since World War II. Polly checks over the new borrowers cards also. Applications must be sent in to the central registration headquarters, where the card is made out and then sent to the branch on the delivery truck. There is also an envelope containing the new regulations governing the circulation of clippings, pictures, and pamphlets. She reads it over, marks several points, and posts it where the rest of the staff will be able to see it.

This job done, Polly checks some of the book orders she is considering. She talks over one or two of them with the other members of the staff, inviting their comments and opinions. One of the long-time patrons of the branch comes in and asks her if she will give a talk on library services to children at the spring meeting of the Parent-Teacher Association which will fall during National Library Week, the nationwide promotion of books and reading held every spring.

Returning to her desk, she starts work on her annual report once more. One of the newest staff members interrupts her. A discussion has arisen at the desk; a patron questions his responsibility for a fine on an overdue book. Polly goes out to the desk and gathers the facts from the patron and from the library records, then settles the matter amicably. While she is there, the adult librarian comes to her with a reference question on which she has been working. She asks Polly for suggestions as to additional sources which she might use to get the necessary information.

The question answered, Polly returns to her desk and puts the report in a folder. She may have to take it home to finish it. She picks up the penciled draft of an annotated reading list she has prepared for the neighborhood newspaper. She reads it over and makes a few corrections before asking the clerk to type it for her.

Requisitions must be signed. This means that the branch supplies have been checked and orders made out for those that need replenishing from the central stock at headquarters. Working against time, she finally snatches her hat and coat, pulls another folder from the file, and takes a hurried leave of the staff. She is due at a meeting at the central library with the chief librarian, the head of extension, the public relations director, and a few others to lay the preliminary plans for the fiftieth anniversary of her branch which will be observed in June. Polly must build up a citizens' committee from her own neighborhood to assist with arrangements. A brainstorming session follows, with many ideas for a suitable program bursting forth from all sides of the table.

When the meeting is over, Polly stops in the book selection room for a brief look at one of the reviewing periodicals. She is still doubtful about one of the books she has on her order list. She would like this particular reviewer's opinion. She reads it over, then goes to the office of the coordinator of adult services to ask her advice. After a short discussion she decides to purchase the title. That point settled, she drives back to the branch, checks to see if the substitute evening schedule is working out, and goes home.

A department head in a large library would have some duties similar to Polly's. He would be responsible for staff schedules, and for the smooth operation of his department. He would select books in a special subject field, a field in which he would be expected to have a wide and authoritative knowledge. He would be responsible for reports, preparation of special book lists, and would, like Polly, be asked to make talks. A department operates as a specialized library within a library. The head, however, is not charged with the maintenance of the physical plant as the head of a separate building is. Nor is he concerned with the registration of borrowers or the charging of library materials. There is a separate department for that with its own head.

The size of a library will determine the specialization of work. As mentioned earlier, in a smaller library the head will be department head, subject specialist, cataloger, reference librarian, and everything else in addition to administrator. In a very large library, the work will be subdivided into many smaller sections with a consequent increase in the number of supervisory positions.

While it is impossible to describe the many types of work in each library, it can be pointed out that the distinction as well as fascination in public library service is the variety of people served and the subjects dealt with. In a public library every member of the public is treated alike, without regard to age, educational background, economic or social standing,

race, color, or creed. A little girl who loves horse stories is
served with as much interest as the clubwoman who is writing
a paper on Africa. The businessman evaluating new markets
in South America receives the same courteous treatment as
the old man who is looking for the poem he remembers from
childhood. A secretary calls to ask how to spell the word
dictated by her boss; an artist designing a layout for the
new airport wants pictures of planes; a recruit to the Great
Books program needs help in looking up a selection from
St. Thomas Aquinas. The minister who is developing a ser-
mon on charity comes in to find quotations and anecdotes to
illustrate his point; the mother of the bride needs assistance
in planning the receiving line for the reception. The foreign
bride of a serviceman shyly asks help in finding books to help
her become an American citizen. A middle-aged man who
missed college wants a reading list to help him fill the gaps
in his background. A teen-ager needs some books on poise
and popularity. They all come to the public library.

County and Regional Libraries

County libraries have been a natural development to serve
people in small towns and in rural areas. However, in some
places, as transportation cuts down on distances and as rural
areas slowly become suburban, city and county libraries lose
their distinction and the city library becomes a county library.

This is not invariably true. The county library which
serves towns and villages, rural schools and individual farms
still is a powerful force in the library world. Leaders in the
profession have long advocated "larger units of service." This
means that instead of each small community trying to maintain its own small library when available funds will not begin

to cover the cost of a professional librarian's salary, much less buy an adequate collection of books or necessary equipment, the communities band together. With pooled resources they establish a centralized library to bring economies in ordering and processing books. The county establishes a library headquarters, opens branches at strategic points in the area, usually making use of existing libraries when possible, and operates bookmobiles to serve the rural areas.

The county library may have a board of citizens just as a city library usually does. It also is a unit of the county government, and receives its operating budget from public funds.

Where a single county cannot support a library, regional libraries are the answer. Here, two or three counties band together and by contract establish a library which serves them all.

The rapid growth of large, heavily populated suburban areas around the large city has created problems for the library as well as other municipal government departments. Many city libraries have become county libraries. Service, organization, and administration are the same as a city library, but the use as well as the financial support is countywide, rather than citywide.

Service in a rural and sparsely populated area will differ from the kind offered in a metropolitan county or region. This does not mean that the quality is lower; but that the service is planned for the area, whether books are dispensed over a desk, by bookmobile, or by mail. In a densely populated area, people will be more likely to come to a library—a county branch or county headquarters. In sparsely populated areas, there will be more reliance on a bookmobile.

As in a city library, a county or regional library has **many** kinds of jobs for the librarian. There will be administrators and children's librarians; there will be reference librarians and branch librarians, and so on through the list of jobs to be done and people to do them. Since bookmobiles are the popular symbol of county libraries although they are also used by city systems, let us look over Ellen's shoulder as she goes about her work as a county bookmobile librarian.

Ellen is in charge of a bookmobile which also carries a driver and a clerk. In some places the librarian may be the driver as well, but Ellen has a complete staff. She is responsible for proper action in case of emergency or accident. Out on the road, her first duty is to help the borrowers at each stop. She may find the books they want; and she tells them about different titles and advises on the selection of "a good story." She answers reference questions from the stock available on the bookmobile if that is possible. If it is not, she adds the questions to the stock of requests for specific titles or information that she takes from the library patrons during the day. These requests will be filled at headquarters and brought to the patrons on the next trip.

Between times, she takes applications for cards if the borrowers are eligible for bookmobile service. Stock on a bookmobile is necessarily limited because of the truck's size, so Ellen is anxious to shelve the books returned at each stop. These books are examined for damage, and any necessary payment made by the patron. Books that are needed to fill special requests are set aside. So are books which are badly worn or in need of repair. They will be sent to the bindery or discarded upon Ellen's return to headquarters.

As the day ends, Ellen is busy making a list of additional books needed for the next trip.

In between these duties the bookmobile crew has had a treat in the form of Amanda Swanson's molasses cookies, just out of the oven as they drove into the farmyard. They have seen the new calf in the Beardsley barn, stopped to eat lunch in a sunny meadow, picked some of the year's first cowslips, and survived the mass visits of two schools.

Ellen has duties at headquarters, too. She chooses the books for each day's trip, keeping in mind the special needs and interests of the people in the locality. She unloads the boxes from the previous trip, distributing the books for shelving, repair, discard, reserves, and so on. She looks for material to answer the requests for information she has received. While this is going on, patrons are using the headquarters library, either in person or by telephone, and Ellen must stop to help them.

She also finds time for book selection. In Ellen's library, each librarian is responsible for a certain area of the book stock, so she concentrates on selecting and ordering books and other materials in science. Each librarian also has certain special individual duties. Ellen schedules the bookmobile trips, assigns the crews, keeps the trip calendar up to date, works with the staff of the two bookmobiles on operational problems, and keeps the bookmobile statistics. With the director and the drivers, she considers the discontinuance of certain stops, where new ones will be established, and the rescheduling of others.

Like the mailman, Ellen braves snow and rain and heat but she would not exchange her post on the library-on-wheels with anyone. If you want to join Ellen in this field of library service you should read the U. S. Department of Agriculture's Farmers' Bulletin, number 2142, called "Library Service for Rural People."

State Agencies

Some kind of state library agency has been established in each of the fifty states. The form of organization and the work of these agencies takes almost fifty forms. A common form of organization is the state library commission made up of lay members who choose a professional director or secretary, or it may be a division of the state Department of Education. The agency may take the form of a state library, or a library department within the state government.

Duties performed by the agencies cover a wide range of possibilities. They may include direct and indirect service or supplementary service to local libraries; the planning and promotion of public and school libraries; a lending service through package or traveling libraries; service to state institutions including prisons and mental hospitals; coordination of the library activities in the state; supervision, administration and counsel; lending of special materials such as films, books in Braille or talking books for the blind. Some agencies might perform all of these functions; some only a very few.

Such activities as direct library service to the state governmental departments and officials; a law library, or legislative reference service; the preservation of historical materials or legislative archives; the distribution and exchange of official documents may be provided by various means. It is quite common to find the law libraries, archives, historical libraries and legislative reference services operated independently of the state library agency.

The state library agency should, of course, administer the agency and all statewide library activities. It helps citizens establish new libraries. It will administer programs resulting from federal and state legislation. A most important function is the coordination of library activities throughout the state and the collection of statistics and information on services and costs of service in the governmental subdivisions. The "state office" is the logical one to call for this type of information. The state library director should be conversant with the library picture in his state and able to relate it to the national picture.

The state agency is the one to supply advisory service to libraries, especially the smaller agencies. To this end, field representatives are frequently attached to the agency, traveling through the state, visiting smaller operations, giving advice and counsel. State agencies plan and sponsor workshops, conferences, and meetings where librarians receive knowledge of new developments in the field and can exchange ideas for their mutual benefit. It may take the lead in establishing such operations as a film circuit, showing small libraries how they can join together, pool their funds, and thereby give their borrowers the benefit of some of the newer and more expensive means of preserving human thought.

Good state agencies are in the forefront in promoting legislation for libraries of all kinds. This removes the legislation from partisan politics and also assures laws which can be applied sensibly and beneficially. They also are important in providing demonstrations of library service. This means that library service—let us say a bookmobile—is provided to an area on a short-term basis so that this community, which has never known a good library, can see what one is and what it would mean to them in their lives and work. Invariably, the community will then take steps to provide itself with its own library service.

Equalization of service is a state agency's concern; that is, it has as a goal the provision of good library service to all the citizens of the state.

A lending service may be operated by the state library agency. This means that citizens without library service write to their state agency and ask to have the books or information they need sent to them. The agency will also arrange for interlibrary loan.

During a day the head of a state library agency might attend a meeting of the state National Library Week committee; testify before a committee of the state legislature regarding the need for proposed library legislation; prepare a statement for a newspaper reporter on the increase of libraries and library service in the state since the passage of the Library Services Act, which produced federal aid for libraries; look over the bids for a bookmobile to be used in demonstration; call home to ask his wife to pack a bag so that he can leave early the next morning for a district conference in the northern part of the state; and end up the day by appearing at a meeting in a nearby town where the citizens are debating whether or not to join the local county library system.

Armed Services Libraries

Serving the country's armed forces—Army, Navy and Air Force—as well as their dependents is a network of libraries here and overseas. Books follow them to training camps, to the various posts throughout the world, on ship, and in time of war, books even find their way to the front. These libraries have branches, deposit collections, even bookmobiles, and maintain programs like those of a public library—discussion groups, forums, exhibits, and so on.

In addition, there are special libraries such as those at the Naval Research Laboratory and Naval Ordnance Laboratory in Washington, D.C., the Air University Library at Maxwell Air Force Base in Alabama, and the Naval Electronics Laboratory at San Diego, California.

One civilian librarian who worked for the armed services abroad said:

In a small library you do everything involved in running a library. "Everything" includes fighting for budget and supplies, ordering and processing books, supervising personnel, publicity, and working with the public. Because of this wide range of activities it is excellent experience and gives you a chance to discover your special interests and abilities. Depending upon where you are stationed you may live on the "local economy" which enables you to get a closer look at the people of the country. And, of course, this kind of job gives you an opportunity to travel.

Overseas Information Libraries

At least 25 million patrons yearly use the 176 United States Information Service libraries and the reading rooms in 80 far-flung countries. Information centers and libraries are the heart of the United States Information Agency's cultural program. The purpose of these overseas posts is to show other peoples that this country's goals and policies are not only in tune with their own hopes for liberty, for peace, and for prosperity but will also help to advance those aspirations. Officers recruited for these posts must be able to give evidence of this fact. They must be equipped to meet hostile propaganda. They must mobilize all available means—press, television, radio, displays, books, motion pictures, and personal contacts in their effort to demonstrate the United States' wish for freedom and for mutual peaceful progress.

To countries who think of libraries as places where books are kept in safety on sequestered shelves for scholars, the free libraries maintained as part of the United States Information Centers with their open shelves, and their information service are revelations. One librarian may sometimes direct the activities of several such libraries, local assistants handling the day-to-day activities. Another activity of the United States Information Agency is to foster binational centers, libraries open to the public but with borrowing privileges usually available only to members and students. These centers are privately sponsored to promote friendship and understanding between the United States and the host country. Assistance comes from the USIA in supplying books and magazines, administrative and teaching personnel, and even cash grants. A professional librarian may be appointed as consultant for a string of such centers, his chief responsibility being assistance in the development of the library program.

The attacks on USIS (United States Information Service) libraries by Communist-ruled countries prove their effectiveness as weapons to combat misunderstanding abroad. Books giving the facts about the American way of life offer such a threat to the Communist party line that there have been many outbreaks of violence against the libraries. A pro-Castro mob set fire to a binational center in Morelia, Mexico, damaging the building so severely that it had to be closed. However, outraged students immediately petitioned the government to restore it.

In his article, "USIA's Library Program in Latin America," Edward R. Murrow, head of the USIA, tells a story of a Communist leader in Honduras, who was motivated largely by reading a book from the USIA to renounce his party membership and denounce the Castro regime. He tells also of the librarian in Panama City who was startled when she looked up from her desk to find a party of colorful Cuna Indians from the San Blas Islands. They had heard of the library and on one of their infrequent trips to town dropped in to "see the books."

Those interested in library positions in the agency should apply to the USIA Information Center Service, Washington 25, D. C. Candidates should have command of at least one foreign language and have a good background as well as a current knowledge in the field of foreign affairs.

Government Libraries

In addition to the libraries for the armed services and the USIS libraries, the federal government maintains many kinds of libraries. Most important, of course, is the Library of Congress, founded to serve Congress but which is also used by other libraries, by scholars and even by the general public. National service in agriculture and related science is given by the Department of Agriculture Library. The Armed Forces Medical Library, charged with research in the field of medicine, is the third federal library giving national service. National Archives is responsible for the preservation and organization of national documents and for making them available for use.

All three branches of the government—legislative, judicial, and executive—have libraries to serve their special needs. Examples are the Senate Library, the House of Representatives Library, the General Accounting Office Library, the Bureau of the Budget Library, the Internal Revenue Bureau Library, the Department of the Interior Library, the Coast and Geodetic Survey Library, the Weather Bureau Library.

Independent agencies also have libraries to serve their special needs. Examples are the scientific research libraries maintained by the Atomic Energy Commission, the Federal Reserve System Library, and the Tariff Commission Library.

There are special collections in the divisions of the Smithsonian Institution and libraries in the Freer and National galleries of art.

While this is only a peek through the crack of the door into the library operations of the government, it serves to illustrate that wherever men are working they need books to help them.

The federal agency handling libraries is the Library Services Branch in the Office of Education of the Department of Health, Education and Welfare. In 1870, the U.S. Bureau of Education included libraries in its annual report. This was the first time that libraries were given a nod of recognition as educational agencies. Almost seventy years later, in 1938, the Library Services Division was established. Under the Library Services Act in 1956 it was reorganized and enlarged. Now about one-half of the staff of the Library Services Branch works on research and statistics; the other in administering the Library Services Act.

College, University, and Research Libraries

The country has some 1,450 rapidly growing college and university libraries. This number can be subdivided into as many kinds as the universities and colleges themselves—state and private, liberal arts colleges, junior colleges, teachers colleges, technical institutes, religious colleges, and so on. They range from the Harvard library with 5,700,000 volumes down to the junior colleges which concentrate on small working collections of up-to-date books geared to the class needs of their students.

Positions in the field would vary also from the librarian at a small college who does everything, to the administrator of a large university library system with several libraries under his direction. Special libraries exist in this field also. For instance, large universities have special libraries for the law school, the medical school, and the agricultural school. There may be an art library, a music library, and so on.

Usually, a college or university library will have a stack area, a reference and reading room, a reserve collection for books assigned for class reading, periodical, newspaper and document sections, a browsing area, and probably a rare book room. In some colleges and universities the rare book collections are notable and a scholar from halfway across the world may journey to a particular one to examine the book and manuscript treasures in his field.

College and university libraries are expanding rapidly. The growth in population is one factor. The increase in enrollment, already felt, is expected to hit its peak in 1970. In addition, the place of books and related materials has taken on a new and different significance in education. Undergraduate students no longer confine themselves to "texts." Rather, their reading ranges widely and they are taught to make comparisons, evaluate, and weigh the evidence they find.

The library's first function in a college and university is to collect, preserve, and make accessible to its own particular users materials tracing the emergence and development of ideas and events in subjects offered at the university.

The building of a college and university library collection is an important responsibility of the librarian. He has, probably, more help from his public than most librarians. Faculty members will supply long lists of books and other materials which must be purchased. The librarian has the job of co-ordinating these musts, fitting them into the program and the budget. He also will know of publications which the scholar may have missed. In addition, the librarian must select all the many materials which are so necessary but which will be neglected by scholars—reference books, serials, periodicals, documents, and similar items would fall in this field. He also has the extremely important task of keeping the collection to a workable size; he must decide on discards, transfers, and so on. With bursting shelves, this problem of the size of the collection has become an important one for colleges and universities. More and more cooperation between institutions has developed, so that all libraries need not collect all subjects and all possible titles. Instead, certain institutions are responsible for the research collections in certain fields. Other libraries know, then, that a copy of a work needed in research in that subject will be available and they can free space accordingly.

More and more the library is also taking an active role in the instructional program. In some cases faculty members have offices in the library, classes meet in the library, and library staff members actually engage in the teaching process.

The university library is a scholarly library. Needs of the undergraduate are not ignored and are usually met by a general collection. The emphasis, however, on both collection and service is directed toward scholarly research. Ernest Hatch Wilkins, a former president of Oberlin College, classified the groups to which a university library offers its collection and services into three. First he placed the mature scholars, which would include the faculty of the university;

second, the "scholars in training," or the graduate and professional students; and third, the undergraduates whom he calls the "potential" scholars. The building must be planned and arranged to meet the needs of the scholar; the collection must be built to serve their present and their future needs; and a staff, sympathetic to the need and value of scholarly research—many of them scholars themselves—must be developed.

On the other hand, a college library cannot exist to serve undergraduates only. It also has a scholarly faculty to serve and frequently some graduate students, although these probably are not beyond the master's level.

College and university libraries, like public libraries, are experiencing a building boom. The librarian will be responsible for plannng a building with the architects, but he must also listen to the needs and the advice of the faculty. The library must be planned to fit the program of instruction and study. Provision must be made for meeting rooms, conference rooms, even classes. There must be carrels or study cubicles where a scholar can pursue a subject in solitude.

The academic atmosphere prevailing upon a campus appeals to many librarians. You are thrown with people who are interested in human thought. Many professors are famous in their field and the opportunity to know them and work with them is a precious one. You are also working with potential scholars, many of whom will also be famous in time. Luminous names in literature, art, music, drama, science, politics are attracted to a campus. Cultural opportunities abound on the calendar. College and university librarians also play an important role in the library world. They are prominent in professional organizations and contribute to the discussion, both oral and written, of the profession.

School Libraries

"Librarians cannot be neutral in the face of change. Nor does a negative attitude contribute to a constructive approach to the future. Librarians should encourage and spearhead the examination of new ideas in education."

These are the words of J. Lloyd Trump, associate secretary of the National Association of Secondary School Principals, in his article in the ALA *Bulletin* for February 1961. He then goes on to describe some of the plans for school libraries of the future. Schools will place responsibility on the student for learning and for the development of intellectual inquiry. They will recognize individual differences in ability as never before. The student will spend more time in independent study, high school students spending as much as twelve hours a week in such study in school. This time will be spent not only in reading but in viewing, listening, using automated learning devices, and in work in laboratories. Books for these students, says Dr. Trump, will be found in three places in the school. A room similar to the present-day library will house the largest collection. It will have a reading room and conference rooms for smaller groups. There will be open stacks which the students can use freely. Reading materials will be available secondly in various laboratories, each of which will concentrate in a special field of study. And finally, they will be found in the individual student cubicles which are used for study so that a student need not go to his locker for them. Films and filmstrips, records and tapes, and various electronic devices will be as important as books and as much a part of the library's business. He says the school librarian will be an expert on "the technology of instruction." He will serve on the teaching team, and the services of the library itself will be the loom on which the school's educational program is woven.

Nor is this so distant a dream. Already high school libraries are subdivided into subject departments. They have records, films, slides, and filmstrips. Individual listening booths, each equipped with its own record player, table, and chair, are found in the new libraries along with preview rooms for films. Microfilmed periodicals and newspapers— once a rarity in large university and public libraries—are now a part of the high school library.

Along with their senior counterparts, elementary school libraries are growing like Jack's famous beanstalk. Parents, concerned with their child's education, are forming citizen committees to urge more and better school libraries. The publication of *Standards for School Library Programs* in 1960 by the American Association of School Librarians, a division of the American Library Association, has startled librarians, school officials, and laymen into recognizing the importance of this area of library service and the need for upgrading state standards.

School libraries have been rechristened "materials centers" to indicate the present stress on the use of many sources of information to educate youngsters at an early age to the need for intellectual inquiry. A world that is sending men into unexplored space needs to develop in its citizens the ability to question, to evaluate, to uncover facts, and to relate them to each other. Present programs of education with the school library as a vital center seek to do this.

A good school librarian and a good teacher work together. While she is planning a unit or before she makes an assignment, the teacher confers with the librarian to find out if there is sufficient material available in the library to meet the needs of her pupils. The librarian suggests new publications, reminds the teacher of works she may have overlooked, and locates articles, maps, pictures, films, slides, and similar materials which will enrich the teacher's classes. Taking a leaf from the book of the White Queen in *Through the Looking Glass*, the school librarian tries to remember the "things that happened the week after next." In other words, she tries to keep well informed on what is going on in the school and what the teachers are planning. She anticipates needs and tries to order materials which will meet them. She makes it her pleasant task to call the attention of a particular teacher to a special publication which will add depth or breadth to her teaching.

What does a school librarian do? That will depend upon the library, and the school, even on the city and the state in which it is located. Every librarian's program will differ from another's. But to give a picture of a high school librarian's day, let us follow Louise Park through an actual page of her diary as she recorded it:

Arrive at 7:15. Post myself at door to check books of people leaving library. Answer questions as to location of books, where to find material, etc., while doing police work. (This is one of the busiest times of the day.)

Move on to charging desk to check in overnight material and to write overdue notices. Check calendar to see who is scheduled to bring classes to library. Route study hall people to proper locations so as to make room for class. Time out for coffee.

Confer with English teacher regarding unit planned: how much material is available and how it can best be used. Make myself available to offer teachers or students any help needed.

Supervise student help so that they will perform duties at circulation desk. Check study hall attendance. Take some time to supervise study hall people.

See salesman who has new encyclopedia to sell. See another salesman who is bidding on furniture for new addition to library.

Time out for lunch.

Work on book order. Consult with clerical worker concerning cataloging problem. Finish list of professional books to be ordered from special funds.

At 2:30 get ready for the last hour of after-school activity at which time students are busily finding material to use in library or to take home for use later.

At 3:30 the library is cleared of the remaining people, the librarians pick up their reading material for the evening, and all is quiet until the next morning at 7:15.

Another school librarian points out that each hour of the day depends upon how many classes come in and how many students from study hall get library passes. If there are many in a single hour it takes all the librarian's time "on the floor," helping both teachers and students find needed materials. She adds: "One doesn't sit down much, ever. All my friends are so surprised when I say I am on my feet practically all day. But being a school librarian is interesting, and funny things happen all of the time."

Hospital and Institution Libraries

Mrs. Macklin plumped up her pillows, settled back comfortably, and opened her book. She wanted to finish it before the librarian's visit. With luck, she could get through another book or two before she went home. She hoped the best seller the girls in the bridge club had been reading would be on the hospital book cart and maybe one of those classics she had always meant to read but never had—like *War and Peace* or *Kristin Lavransdatter*. The mother of four—the last one only two days old—she looked forward to these trips to the hospital for a little time to herself to read and rest and relax.

Up on another floor, Mr. Staley smiled a little wryly. That little librarian was a sharp one all right. She must have seen how depressed he had been after the doctor told him about his heart. She had insisted on leaving a slim volume for him. He had read it in spite of himself and he had to admit that things didn't look quite so black afterward.

In the small library room, Kitty Chester had Mrs. Macklin and Mr. Staley in mind as she loaded her book cart, ready for her first trip of the day to the patients of the big hospital. Employed by the city's public library, Kitty served three hospitals. This one was so large she spent two days a week here, giving the other two one day's service. On the fifth day she went to the central library to select books and gather material to answer the reference questions she had been asked.

Hospital library service is organized in many different ways, depending upon the city, the hospital, and the administration responsible for it.

In the recruiting pamphlet, "A Rewarding Career Is Waiting for You in Hospital Librarianship," the Association of Hospital and Institution Libraries of the American Library Association points out that five kinds of library service are developing:

> *Medical,* which depends for its goals and its scope on the clinical, educational and research program of the hospital as well as its specialty.
>
> *Nursing,* which implements the curriculum in hospitals with the schools of nursing.
>
> *Patients,* the type in which Kitty was engaged and which is the oldest in concept.

Administrative, which is the newest type and increasing in importance in all hospitals.

Integrated, which integrates and organizes the four types above under professional librarianship.

The Veterans Administration has a well-developed library program for hospitalized veterans and for a medical library program serving the medical personnel in veterans hospitals. The description of the librarian's functions in dealing with patients as given in "The Librarian in the Veterans Administration" (pamphlet 10-41, available from the Veterans Administration, Washington 25, D. C.) is a good one:

Aids recovery through the dissipation of idleness, contentment of mind, and assistance in the patients' psychological adjustments.

Participates in programs using books and periodicals as part of the total therapy, when medically directed.

Gives reader's advisory service to patients with varied backgrounds and interests, including preparation of lists and planned reading courses especially for long-term patients.

Minimizes the patient's concern with his hospitalization by furnishing him materials which not only aid him to understand his limitations but also allow him to live up to the brink of his capabilities.

Helps the patient to adjust to new working or living conditions by supplying materials which are the informational tools needed to cope with unfamiliar problems.

These librarians make visits to the wards with book carts and for some patients they employ such aids as the projected book which will show a filmed book on the ceiling, allowing an immobile patient to read it. Talking book machines play recorded books. Prismatic glasses allow a patient to read without raising his head. Page turners and reading tables are other aids for handicapped readers.

In this type of hospital, where there are ambulatory patients, the librarian may organize discussion groups, Great Books groups, and other activities. One librarian experimented with a poetry reading circle for mentally disturbed patients.

Quite different from the hospital librarian's job is that of the medical librarian in the Veterans Administration. As a member of the hospital team she works with doctors, dentists, nurses, technicians, and other specialists. The same VA pamphlet lists the duties in this way:

> You will assist and further the education, reading, and research program of the professional staff of the hospital.
>
> You will, conjointly with the staff, select and maintain a collection of up-to-date, scientific literature to meet the requirements of the staff in studying and providing constantly improved patient care.
>
> You will render bibliographic, reference, and inter-library loan services.
>
> You will instruct library clientele in the use of the catalog and the special reference tools and indexes.

If you are interested in an appointment to the library service of the Veterans Administration, you can procure an appointment blank from your nearest Veterans Administration installation, a first- or second-class post office, or the U.S. Civil Service Commission regional office which serves your area.

A nursing school library has the same function as a college library, serving in the specialized field of nursing. Like a college library, too, it must supply the students—in this case student nurses—with the materials they need to meet the reading and reference requirements of the curriculum. Again like a college library, it must serve graduates and instructors so it has reference materials for graduate nurses and the nursing school faculty. Some nursing school libraries also offer non-curricular reading. In a large city, the nursing school librarian may arrange field trips to the city library to introduce the students to its facilities so that they have the opportunity to gain a wider cultural background.

Closely allied to service to hospitals is the library service to institutions such as those for the blind and for the mentally retarded. One of the fields in which there should be increasing development and one in which there is a growing awareness of the need is that of library service to penal institutions. Prisons with adequate library collections and professional librarians are not the general rule. Librarians as well as penologists are working for full recognition of the importance of books in the treatment of the sentenced offender.

Special Libraries

The librarian was finishing her dessert and coffee with a few fellow staff members in the cafeteria.

"I never could understand why they call them 'special' libraries," she said. "All libraries are special in some way. Look at the art department—that's a special library. Look at the music library over at the university—that's special. Hospital service is special. What makes special libraries 'special'?"

Special libraries *are* found in almost every kind of organization. They are information centers in a particular subject field and the patrons are a limited group who make use of the library and its collection for the specific conduct of their business or research.

Because of the limited subject field and consequent limited clientele, special librarians are likely to have a much closer association with the work of their patrons. They keep the library users informed of new publications in their particular fields of interest, and abstract articles for them.

There is a common tendency to think of special libraries as libraries for business or industry. It is true that there are many libraries in these fields—in insurance companies, banks, law firms, newspapers, advertising agencies, and in firms manufacturing everything from electronic diodes to typing paper. Just as special are the subject departments in public and university libraries, or the libraries of the various government bureaus, the many kinds of museums, and the business and professional associations. Even the American Library Association maintains a special library—a library dealing with libraries as its subject.

Museums—art, science, natural history, historical, and the like—frequently maintain libraries in their subjects. Theological and religious libraries are important fields. Seminaries, schools of theology and divinity, make serious use of printed materials. The theater claims that libraries in its field date back to the famous Alexandrian library. Atomic energy, space, and other unfolding worlds of science offer new and exciting opportunities for the special librarian.

Special libraries are developing much faster in the field of automation than their sisters in the public library field. The smaller collections and the type of material handled adapt

well to the new methods for locating information with automated equipment discussed in Chapter 11. Also, science,
business, and industry are usually better equipped financially to handle such a program than the public institution.

Characteristic of special librarians is a high sense of
enthusiasm for their work. Their conferences offer stimulating programs. Their association issues its own magazine,
Special Libraries, at 31 East 10th Street, New York 3,
N. Y., which gives a good picture of the field to one interested
in entering it. Examination of several issues would give an
idea of the philosophy, work, and aims of this branch of
library service.

SEVEN

The Field: Types of Work

HE WAS NOT very tall. A little boy's spiky, uncombed hair stuck out from under his red knitted cap. His long-lashed brown eyes were big in the round face dirt-streaked from after-school play.

"Do you have *Inki*?" The brown eyes looked up hopefully at the librarian, surrounded by boys and girls. She turned from the shelves where she had been looking for books on dinosaurs for a trio of youngsters.

"Let's see. *Inki*—that's a dog story, isn't it?"

"No, it's a children's story."

Children's Librarians

Incidents like this enliven the life of every librarian who works with children. They work with the age group which has not yet discovered that it is too busy to read. Their patrons move into a book and live there with the characters while they read it. It is an age of belief, of wonder, and of intense curiosity about everything—stars and stamps, cavemen and astronauts, King Arthur and Mickey Mantle, radio and carrier pigeons, skin diving and horned toads, saints and outlaws.

124

Children's librarians also deal with adults. There are the parents, grandparents, aunts, and uncles, who want advice on guiding the reading of their particular children, grandchildren, nieces, and nephews, who want suggestions for books to borrow or for books to buy. Sometimes these problems are very specific—a child who is a slow reader and needs something to interest him; another who has a one-track mind and will read nothing but books on baseball; one who should have more imaginative literature.

Then there are the adult reference questions which must be answered from children's sources. An artist is making designs for memo pads and would like to see woodcuts from old primers. A firm developing a large shopping center asks for illustrations of animals to be used to designate the various sections of their mammoth parking lot. The head of a laundry service wants several editions of *Snow White and the Seven Dwarfs*; the little princess will be the trademark for the snowy linens he handles. An advertising copywriter, seeking a new theme for a line of children's clothing, asks for fairy tales, Roman history, and Bible stories, hoping they will spark his imagination.

Children's librarians have many opportunities to talk to adult groups also. Church organizations, parent-teacher associations, and groups of youth leaders such as those for Boy Scouts, Girl Scouts, Campfire Girls, and so on turn to them for talks on children's books and reading.

But the largest public of the children's librarian is composed of youngsters up through junior high school age. She helps to start toddlers, even infants, on the book road with picture books, nursery rhymes, and finger games. She is the first to recognize, regretfully, that an eager youngster's abilities and needs have gone beyond the children's room and he must be sent on to the adult departments.

Something of the actor should dwell in every children's librarian. Highly prized are the story hours where bright-eyed youngsters sit on the floor following the storyteller as she goes from page to page, showing the bright-colored illustrations and narrating the tale. This same talent is useful in the many outlets available on radio and television.

To many children her visits to their schoolroom are among the delightful surprises of the year. Her talk about the library and the story she tells with a promise that there are more like it in the children's room, tease their appetites. Many of them will come to see her on their way to the skating rink or the ball field when classes are over.

The children's librarian should have many of the show-man's instincts besides that of the performer. She must have an eye for the dramatic in exhibits, a flair for selecting a performer. Puppet shows put on either by staff, the young patrons, or by "outside" talent are common. Special surprises in the way of decoration, display, and entertainment are part and parcel of Children's Book Week, Christmas, Spring Book Festival, and other special days on the library calendar.

The children's librarian is concerned, too, with helping children to find better and better books; to start them on new roads of discovery. This is in her mind in the selection of books for the collection. She must know her books exceptionally well for when a child wants to know what a book is about he means just that—all about it.

The books she handles are a special dividend in children's work. In this field there are so many examples of beautiful illustrations, color, design, and typography. It means that she has about her some of the most interesting examples of bookmaking. In some libraries, she will also be privileged to become acquainted with juvenile publishing in other countries, for a collection of foreign books, once a nice extra in children's rooms, is becoming more of a necessity as the world shrinks and as American schools put greater emphasis on the early learning of foreign languages.

Some of the most dramatic events in the library world occur in the children's field. One is the annual choice of the best book for children published in the United States in the preceding year and also of the best illustrated picture book. The first will receive the Newbery Medal and the second the Caldecott Medal, given by Frederic Melcher of the R. R. Bowker Company. Announced in the spring, the medals are formally presented at the annual conference of the American Library Association at a gala dinner. Usually the author and the illustrator who win the medals are present, their acceptance talks giving the audience an unforgettable picture of their work and ideals.

Many opportunities for professional exchange are offered in this field. The state library association usually contains an active section for children's librarians. On the national level the Children's Services Division of the American Library Association not only undertakes many ambitious projects of benefit to children's librarians and children's literature, but also offers a friendly forum for exchange of ideas, problems and solutions with colleagues around the nation.

Avenues for promotion for children's librarians are increasing. In large systems there is usually someone who coordinates all children's services in the central library and the extension agencies. This is an obvious goal and a position of importance and responsibility. Children's librarians also have opportunities for advancement as branch library heads.

They can turn to school library service where promotion lies in supervisory positions. Not infrequently they are taken from the active library ranks by publishing houses to act as juvenile editors.

Work with Young Adults

An outsider, looking at the intralibrary memos of a large system, might become confused as he picked out notices of meetings of young adult librarians and adult librarians. He might think that here, indeed, was a profession whose members were slow in maturing or else one which recruited people at an early age. To a librarian there is no problem here. Young adult librarians are the ones who deal with readers from approximately fifteen years old to college age. They designate their field simply as "YA."

One of the most important tasks of any YA librarian is book selection. Juvenile publishing must be watched for teen-age books appropriate to the young adult level. Adult books must be carefully appraised to select those titles which are of special interest to this age level. It is in this period that young people find so many interests competing with reading for their spare time. Books in a collection for them must be fresh and attractive, truly "bait" to catch the capricious nibbler.

A librarian for young adults spends a good amount of time in advising readers. She will make book lists to help them in their selection, but she also spends time on the floor to give personal assistance. Follow one on the floor after school. You will hear girls ask:

"Can you give me a good book?"

"I'm looking for a teen-age romance."

"I just love Mary Stewart's novels! But I've read them

all. Are there any others just like them?"

Boys will follow her, too, asking:

"Is there a hot rod story in today?"

"*Kon-Tiki* was great! Did that author write anything else?"

"Say, I want some new science fiction. Is there anything in? And something on World War II, if you've got it—preferably anything written by a G.I. in Europe or the South Pacific."

That terrifying experience—facing an assembly of high school students and trying to interest them in what you have to say—is another big job. In this field especially, the library must go out to its patrons and convince them that books, films, periodicals, and pictures have something they want and need. Within the library walls as well, the librarian must challenge the young person's interest. Discussion groups have proved successful in some areas. Special events such as book shows, an evening with the city's professional baseball team, afternoons with an author, attract the busy high-schooler. In some cities a library council made up of selected representatives from all the high schools has been a popular and a profitable aid to the librarian in planning activities.

Like the children's librarian, a librarian for young adults has requests from parents and teachers as well as students. Parents will say anxiously:

"We'd like to get our son to read something besides the things he has to read for school."

Or, "All my boy will read is science fiction. Isn't there some way to get him to branch out and broaden his interests?"

Teachers will drop in to see the collection and talk it over with the librarian before assigning supplementary reading. They should make sure before making the assignment that there is sufficient material to satisfy every student's need. For instance, if the English teacher has over a hundred students in his classes and asks every one of them to read *A Tale of Two Cities* by a week from Wednesday, he is asking the impossible for school and public library combined will not be able to fill the demand. It is also important for the librarian to be told in advance that there will be an onslaught of young people asking for material on Ghana so that the resources in the library can be parceled out on an equitable basis. The librarian can also help the teacher in their conferences by suggesting books, periodicals, films, and other materials with which the teacher may not be acquainted.

Library school students are always frequent library patrons. They make their way to the young adult librarian for help in building reading ladders, for instance. A reading ladder is a list of books to help the reader raise his reading level gradually, book by book.

High school librarians will spend their professional day working with young people and with their teachers. Theirs is a different relationship from that of the public librarian. They will be engaged primarily in supplying young people with curriculum-related materials to help them become intellectual adventurers as they learn. In many instances, both types of librarians will do both types of work, but the emphasis will be different. Just as a young adult librarian in the public library down the street will have occasion to help a student get materials he needs for an assignment, so will the high school librarian have occasion to introduce him to books for entertainment and recreation. The difference lies in the primary goal of each library and each librarian.

The Young Adult Services Division of the American Library Association is the professional group where librarians in this field find guidance, inspiration, and a chance to exchange information and ideas. With the Children's Services Division, this group issues a quarterly publication called *Top of the News*. Similar groups can be found in state associations.

As in the children's field, large library systems have coordinators of young adult services, a person in charge of advising on the book collection and selection, who counsels the other YA librarians on the staff, who gives talks, and arranges for exhibits and special programs, who seeks new avenues for interesting young adults in the library and for serving them. Young adult librarians also have opportunities to advance as branch librarians, to go on to other libraries, to enter the publishing field.

Services to Adults

Some years ago a popular definition of a public library was "the people's university." The term does indicate one of the library's noblest functions—to provide for the continuing mental development of the adult.

The public library is not the only library which deals with adults. It is obvious that special, college, and research libraries will also have an adult clientele. As a librarian who works with adults you will never lack for variety or for spice in your daily life.

You help the night club entertainer who is investigating the traits, habits, and personality of whales for her act.

You are asked by a young married couple for books on how to get along with other people. They confide that they are moving in with the husband's parents until he gets a better job.

A young couple in a happier situation who have been com-

pletely redecorating their house with the help of library
books and magazines come in to tell you they have finished
the kitchen and it is a great success. Now they are starting
to bleach all the woodwork in the rest of the house. What
can you give them to show how to do it?

A missionary bound for Ecuador wants to spend the weeks
before his departure studying the Quechua Indians. He asks
you to give him a list of books on their history, customs, and
religious beliefs.

The week before you had given a woman a general book
on philosophy. Now she has become so interested in the subject she asks you to start her out on a course of reading on
the lives of philosophers, ancient and modern.

A first-generation American brokenly confides that her
children who are now growing up have become ashamed of
her accent. Can you give her some materials to help her with
her English?

But adult librarians do more than wait behind a desk for
people to come and ask them for help. Like their colleagues
in the children's and young adult field, they also are engaged
in the serious business of selecting the right books, the right
films, the right periodicals for their clientele.

They go out to find their customers as well. They give book
talks or talks about library services to service clubs, luncheon
clubs, study clubs, church circles, and civic groups. They
serve on boards and committees, join associations, and cooperate with civic projects, offering such library services as
appropriate exhibits, lists, meeting rooms, and information
whenever such offers are appropriate and possible.

Meanwhile, back at the ranch which is their own particular
library, they are planning activities to bring in the adults.
Lectures and film programs, recorded or live concerts,

theater readings, tours, discussion groups, even classes in some places. Noon hour programs to catch the businessman and woman are planned. Special activities for parents, or for club chairmen, or for social workers may be offered.

While there are many divisions and round tables in the American Library Association which will attract and serve adult librarians, there is one specifically labeled Adult Services Division which concerns itself with the services which contribute to the "continuing educational, recreational, and cultural development of adults in all types of libraries."

Avenues for promotion for the adult librarian are many. This background combines well with administrative ability to produce a good candidate to head a library—large or small—or to become a branch librarian or department head. More and more libraries of any size are placing adult services under a coordinator who becomes responsible for their effectiveness throughout the system. Subject specializations offer promotions to librarians in the adult field and also chances to change fields; that is, they may transfer from a public to a special library, a college library, or to the armed services libraries. If he wishes to leave the field, the adult librarian may also find opportunities in the publishing business, either on the editorial or the sales side.

Senior Adult Services

In 1930, 5.4 per cent of the population was sixty-five years old or older. Thirty years later this figure had grown to 9 per cent, with some 16½ million persons in this category. Women predominate in this group. They now number 8½ million compared to 7 million men. This preponderance will increase in the next few decades.

No librarian should judge a person's reading tastes or

ability by his age. Because a person reaches sixty-five it does
not mean that overnight his interest in a particular subject,
his liking for certain types of books, will change. Then why
are libraries concerning themselves more and more with the
senior citizen?

The figures given above explain that concern just as they
explain the concern of the government, social agencies, the
church, and similar groups. People are living longer. Those
agencies which serve the public must be conscious of the fact
that there are an increasing number who are living to an
advanced age and they must assume the responsibility for
making that advanced age pleasurable and profitable.

The librarian who chooses this responsibility as his will
realize that the library has much to offer the older person.
Its collection represents all reading levels. Both the man
with little education and his brother with a college degree
can find the things that suit them. Because educational advances affect the young, there are likely to be more people
in the senior group whose level of schooling is below the average for the rest of the population. The librarian must balance the collection so that there will be interesting, attractive, and rewarding books for those whose need and desire
exceeds their reading skill.

As a librarian for older people you will appreciate one of
the library's greatest assets for your patrons: it requires no
degrees, no academic prerequisites. It does not inquire as to
color or creed. Its hours are flexible and so is its program. It
can be enjoyed by the shy and quiet as well as the poised and
self-confident. It offers itself to the individual as well as the
group. You, in turn, will offer individual reading guidance
to the man or woman who suddenly finds more time to pursue
a favorite hobby or interest. You will plan group activities

for those who seek to talk to others through group discussion, to travel far on film, to relive youthful days by means of recorded concerts, or to gain a feeling of fellowship.

You will realize that while a person's brain may be as active and as agile as it ever was, time may dim his eye, rheumatism cripple his hands, or arthritis weaken his grip. For them you will look for books in large and clear type, for good stories that are light to carry and easy to hold.

One of your most important functions as a librarian for senior citizens is to coordinate community activities. You must be careful not to duplicate activities already well covered by some other agency.

Where specific types of programs for the senior citizen are already operating, the library should look for ways in which they can aid the program. If needed services are not offered and they fall within its scope of service, the library can do well to sponsor such programs itself. Effective workshops for agencies engaged in helping older people have been offered by some libraries as a community service. An important field in which the library can either lead by operating its own program or cooperate by supplying materials to another sponsor is that of planning for retirement: income management, housing, health, food, hobbies, employment. Libraries which provide services to shut-ins or to rest homes are working largely for the older man or woman.

The librarian who is working with people in this age bracket needs a lively imagination and sensitive perception. Because a person who reaches sixty-five remains an intelligent human being with the same tastes, interests, and emotions that he had as a young man, his use of the library must not be confined to a "room for aged readers." Rather, the total library program must be examined, and the librarian for senior adults must see where it can offer particular attractions and helps to the older library user. This librarian must also go outside the walls to find the men and women who may not have found the library in their youth but who could make good use of it now that more time is available. To them the library must advertise, showing them a product that will make life richer and more enjoyable.

Armed Forces

The job of the librarian in the armed forces has been described in Chapter Six. This type of library has a section of its own in the American Library Association under the Public Library Association. One army librarian emphasized the great variety this field offers, not only in work but in patrons. She pointed out that one outfit may be chiefly college graduates, interested in imaginative literature, philosophy, history and similar topics, while another may be made up of skilled craftsmen looking for practical materials in applied sciences and in mechanics. A librarian in the armed services may have several libraries under his supervision, thus giving him experience in administration as well as direct service to readers.

Reference Services

The letter was in Russian and had been censored. It was addressed to the mayor of a midland city, who sent it on to the city librarian. He in turn assigned it to the reference department. There one of the librarians, who was studying Russian, combined her knowledge with that of a patron who also knew the language, to produce a translation.

The writer was Sergeant A. His mother, two sisters, and his brother had been killed in the war. He himself had lost a leg and was living in a home for invalid soldiers. "To organize a more normal life," he wrote, he needed some help. He had no relatives in Europe. Years before, about 1926, his father had decided to come to the United States. Everything was ready for the trip, including his visa, when he had suddenly died. His guarantor had been the sergeant's uncle. The sergeant did not remember the uncle's first name, only that he lived in this midwestern city and that he had been in the automobile business. "I turn to you," the letter concluded, "to help me find my uncle."

The reference librarians set to work. They combed the city directories until, in one dated several years before, they found a man named A in the auto business. A check in a current directory uncovered the name of the person who now lived at Mr. A's former address. A telephone call there started another chain of events. The people who had bought the house did not know A's whereabouts but they thought they knew someone who did. Another series of calls located a friend of A's. Yes, he had moved to Florida, but the friend did not know which city. The reference librarians turned to directories again, this time of Florida. In the one for Miami they found Mr. A, still in the automobile business. Off went an airmail letter from the library explaining the situation and asking if Mr. A was the sergeant's uncle. Back flew a letter from Florida. This was indeed the right family, and if the library would forward the soldier's letter they would begin immediate steps to bring him to a new life in the United States. With a feeling of satisfaction the librarians turned to a new problem.

To many people reference work means looking up an item in the encyclopedia. To a good librarian reference work is a combination of detective work and adventure. Completion of a successful search gives him the same sense of excitement and discovery that Balboa must have felt when he topped the mountain range in Panama and saw the sparkling waters of the Pacific.

Students who come to a library—public, school, or college—need reference materials. Part of the librarian's job is to introduce them to reference tools, and to show them how to use these important sources of information. The questions students pose range all the way from the date the Declaration of Independence was signed to the emotional factors affecting an astronaut. In serving students the librarian's primary job is to show them *how* to find what they want, since that is a part of their education, and frequently the purpose of an assignment.

The selection of materials for reference and research is also the reference librarian's job. As in any other branch of library service, this selection is based on the people the library serves, the goals of this particular library, and the money available. In this field you will be handling dictionaries—not just the familiar ones you knew at home and school—but dictionaries of slang, of fable, of color, of science, of professions and trades, of sports, of fungi, and many other subjects. In the same way there are encyclopedias—encyclopedias of the social sciences, of religion and ethics, and the widely varied and often beautiful foreign encyclopedias. You will be looking for and buying directories of every imaginable type, maps and gazetteers, catalogs and bibliographies, handbooks and yearbooks, indexes and directories, compendiums and Who's Who's. Until you actually begin to look at reference books and *see* them, you never realize how many people have labored to put information and clues to information into handy guides for others. You never realize that you can find adventure in a catalog as well as a novel—if the fact you are looking for is there.

Reference librarians are also alert to books not classified as reference tools but which will supply needed information for their clients. A book on international politics may contain good charts of the many new governments formed since World War II as well as biographical sketches of the new national leaders; a pamphlet issued in connection with a local bank's hundredth anniversary may be an excellent survey of the city's history; a book of sports and games may have the rules so often asked for, the dimensions of every kind of playing field. Newspapers and periodicals are indispensable to the reference librarian, and to the clientele he serves.

Reference librarians are interested, too, in the creation of new tools to help them help their patrons. They suggest needed reference books to publishers. They also compile bibliographies and lists in addition to building their own special indexes. Some of these, begun as a simple card file by some librarian who wanted to be able to serve people better and faster, find their way into print and are bought by libraries everywhere for the same purpose.

The group in the American Library Association which is concerned with this area of librarianship is the Reference Services Division.

Behind-the-Scenes

If a library is to have books on its shelves, if it is to have films and records, maps and pictures, periodicals and newspapers, someone must choose them and someone must order them. If they are to be readily accessible so that the public can borrow them and the librarian can find them to answer the patrons' requests they must be classified, arranged, and indexed in a serviceable system.

In a small library *the* librarian may do most of the work involved in all three processes. As the library grows, more and more people will be needed to keep up with the flow of materials and the job will be subdvided into many, the processes becoming more specialized.

Over 15,000 books are published in a year in the United States alone. To this output must be matched the funds available in a given library. The smaller the book budget, the more carefully must the books and other materials be selected. Book selection has always been considered one of a librarian's most important functions. Many aids are available to him—book reviewing services, book reviewing journals, specialized bibliographies and catalogs, magazines which have highly respected book reviewing sections, and so on. In addition, he must have a good background in books, a grounding in the principles of literary criticism. In a special library he should know the literature of the field.

From the tremendous output of publishing, a library must choose the materials it will add to its collection. The publications offered must be considered in the light of the public this library serves—what are they asking for now, what can they be expected to want and need, what should be added to build up the collection's permanent value and usefulness? The library must buy for the present, yes; it must also buy for the future, evaluating the books, noting trends, prophesying what it will need to be of use to its clientele fifty or a hundred years hence. Every library has this problem— the special library, the college library, the research library, the public library, the school library. Each one has different publics, different needs to consider, different long-term goals, but the basic job is the same.

The evaluation done, the selection must be weighed against the budget. Here the librarian is faced with an agonizing decision. What needed title must be dropped because of insufficient funds? In making this decision he knows that some titles, unless they are bought when they are published, soon go out of print and an item of long-term value to the library's patrons may be lost forever.

Too, the librarian will be accused of censorship, of being too liberal or too conservative, too far to the right or too far to the left, of bigotry and of bias. The same librarian may be accused of all of these. This is because the librarian's objective is to see that serious, well-grounded works on all sides of a question are represented on the shelves. Persons who want only their side represented will misunderstand this point of view. It is part of the librarian's job to state and abide by a well-expressed and truly professional policy of selection, one approved by the library board.

Once selected, the books must be ordered. In some libraries the order librarian may be responsible for book selection in certain areas. In any library, because he sees many of the book salesmen, advertisements, publishers' publicity and similar trade news outlets, he should be alert to significant publications and share the responsibility of seeing that the library gets the important items it needs.

Before books are ordered, the library files must be checked to see that the titles are not already in the library or on order. Often the bibliographical work is done by the order librarian; that is, the search for the publisher and his address, the date the work was published, whether or not the book is one of a series, and similar information.

Then he looks for dealers who can give his library the best service and the best discount. It is his responsibility to acquire at the lowest possible cost the books, pamphlets, periodicals, and other materials the library needs but, in so doing, service must not be sacrificed. Such materials must be ready for use promptly by the public which is waiting for them.

For out-of-print books—books no longer available from the publisher—he will start a hunt through secondhand book dealers. In some cases—this happens frequently in the rare book field—this may be a search to rival that of the most adventurous private investigator as he trails an elusive item from place to place.

Financial accounting and reporting are important in this field. An alert librarian is always looking for new methods of simplifying and speeding up all order processes. In a small library the systems may be fairly uncomplicated. In a large system with many branches and many departments, the records are more complex. To keep on top of the necessary paper work, methods must be developed which will keep the *process* from impeding the *result*—the prompt ordering, delivery, and library use of the book.

Records must be organized so that the order librarian can know what is on order and what has been received. Periodicals and certain types of books which come regularly on subscription require elaborate files to tell from whom and when a book was ordered, the date it was received, what it cost, when the bill was received, and to what department the item should go when cataloged.

Delivered to the library, cleared in the order department, the book goes on to the catalog department. There it must be classified. In most cases, a library will use either the Dewey decimal or the Library of Congress classification. The classifier decides in what subject to class this title so that it will stand on the shelves with other books in the same field

waiting to be of the greatest use to the greatest number
of potential users. If a book is an elementary handbook of
arithmetic, a book on the stars, or the collected poems of
Robert Frost, this is a simple decision. But other volumes
pose more complex decisions: should a personal narrative of
a Marine in World War II be classified in biography or in
history? A little book on gymnastics can be a brow wrinkler.
If it relates more to exercise, then it is classified in the 600's;
if it approaches the subject from the angle of athletics it
must go with sports in 700.

There are other decisions to be made. Sometimes the catalog department must find out the author. Should the book
be entered under the name on the title page which may be a
pseudonym or under the author's real name? Sometimes
there is no author on the title page; then who is responsible
for the book? Two authors may have the same name or the
subject of the book may be a man whose name is a common
one. The authors and subjects must be clearly designated
in the catalog so that the library user will find the exact one
he wants, so dates are hunted up and verified. Catalog departments keep an authority file in which they record the
decisions they make on names, on dates, and on other entries.

Subject headings are a problem, too. Every library
chooses and follows a standard guide, adapted to its purposes. But new problems arise. New countries, new subjects
of knowledge, new events—these are common puzzlers to the
cataloger. For instance, when World War II started in 1939,
no librarian could forecast that it would be a "world war."
Germany started on the march and books appeared on the
subject which had to be added to the catalog. The conflict
grew and the books on it were gradually grouped under the
heading "European War, 1939—." Finally, all of them
had to be gathered up and entered under the name that the

war finally became known by, "World War 1939-1945."

Classification and cataloging has an international flavor. Conferences on cataloging draw librarians from many nations as they seek to work out uniform rules so that scholars may find material easily in any library they consult. In recent years, catalogers have been at work revising the cataloging code. A conference on this subject resembles a small United Nations.

The heavy responsibility for such activities as "acquisition, identification, cataloging, classification, and preservation of library materials; and the development and coordination of the country's library resources" is lodged with the Resources and Technical Services Division of the American Library Association. There are special sections in the division for librarians concerned with acquisitions and another for the catalogers and classifiers.

Good persons in any of the behind-the-scenes activities stand in a favorable position for promotion. They must have a good sense of order and because of their concern with the business end of the library and much of its routines they get a good grounding in its operation. They become candidates for administrative posts if they combine awareness of people and an ability to deal with them along with their professional ability. Librarians who spend the major part of their time on book selection acquire an invaluable knowledge of the book world which, when combined with an articulate voice or a facile pen, can bring them recognition on the platform and in print.

Administration

Usually when you are in grade school you discover the old saw, "Even a pin must have a head to be useful." You chant it as a gleeful insult to your small classmates. It takes some experience to find out that the ancient sage who phrased the thought had packed a good deal of wisdom into the ten short words.

A human body certainly needs a head in order that the other parts of the body may operate. To a corporate body—an organization—a head is equally necessary, a head to make the various parts work together in harmony to produce the needed action.

Libraries need heads as well. What does the head of a library do? Usually in ascertaining the meaning of anything it is best to go first to the dictionary. Webster says "to administer" is "to manage or direct the execution, application, or conduct of" an operation. The job of a library administrator will vary with the type of library—public, college, university, school, or special; with the size of the library; with its policy and aims; and with the external factors governing its operation—the community served, local laws, traditions, and the like.

However, some idea of what a head librarian does can be seen from this description of a day in the life of Chris Hollister, the director of a medium-sized library.

He parks his car in the rear of the library and talks briefly with the building superintendent about the problem of removing the ice from the gutters. Arriving at his desk, he starts to go over his calendar with his secretary when the telephone rings. The city purchasing agent is preparing to advertise for bids for a new bookmobile and has a question on the specifications which the library had sent to him.

The morning mail has arrived and Chris goes through it. There is a letter from the buildings and equipment section of ALA's Library Administration Division asking him if he can bring the plans for the addition to the central library to the conference in June. The chamber of commerce sends him an invitation to appear on a forthcoming program to discuss the future of the library in an age of space. He frowns over a sharp letter from a woman who claims that one of the staff was rude to her. He makes a note to get to the bottom of the question and find out from both sides what happened.

Some letters asking for answers to reference questions he sends on to the proper staff members to answer. He sighs as he opens a short communication from the board of control telling him the library budget will be considered at the July meeting. Will he please be ready to present it?

His secretary announces that the librarian who applied for the job of head of reference services has arrived for her interview. He is anxious to get a good person to fill this post, so he greets the visitor hopefully. This interview is followed by one with the librarian who selects the fiction. She has a controversial novel in hand. She has read it herself and has doubts about the wisdom of buying it. Staff reviewers to whom she has given it differ radically in their opinions as do the professional reviewers. Will he please read it to see what he thinks? He takes the book and asks his secretary to put it with his hat and coat so he will not forget to take it home.

Another telephone call is from a reporter on the evening paper. There has been a report that the library plans to discontinue two of its branches. He wants to verify the report and find out the reasons behind the contemplated action if it is true. Chris launches into a patient explanation of the library's financial condition and says that the plan to close two branches is only one of many possible economies the library board is considering in order to balance its budget. No immediate action is foreseen on any of them, especially if the library receives an increase in its next year's budget.

He rings for his secretary and begins to dictate the docket for the next board meeting, a preliminary draft which will be reviewed with the president of the board the next day.

As he dictates the last sentence, she reminds him that today is his Rotary luncheon and he must hurry to get there. At lunch he is pounced on by the head of one of the city's banks who lives in a suburb and is interested in establishing a library there. He asks for advice on how to go about it. As a result of the conversation, he invites Chris to come to the citizens meeting which his committee will call in the next few weeks. He asks Chris to give a talk on the value of a library to a growing community—culturally, educationally, and economically.

From the luncheon Chris drives to one of the branches to go over the possibilities of remodeling an old sunporch into a room for young adults. He and the branch librarian pace off the area, discuss materials, colors, furniture, equipment, and probable costs. He asks her to draft a memorandum outlining the plan and to send it to him for discussion with the building committee of the board.

Back at his desk he is greeted by a committee from the staff association which is working out plans for the annual staff institute. This year the day will be devoted to public relations. They would like to invite an expert from a library in a neighboring state. They ask him if he knows her, her work, and, most important, has he heard her speak? He is enthusiastic about the choice and volunteers to add his invitation to theirs if they think it would have any value.

The head of the circulation department is waiting to catch

him as the committee leaves. She thinks some of the rules are
in serious need of revision. For instance, she points out, their
library is still asking for "references" from people applying
for library cards. She thinks it would be better to request
"identification." Chris promises to appoint a small committee
and set up a meeting next week to consider the problem.

The payroll must be examined and signed. He approves
the bills waiting for his signature before they can be paid.
One of them reminds him that he has an appointment at a
nearby firm to see a demonstration of a book copying
machine. He finishes the bills and hurries to keep the engage-
ment. He spends some time watching the salesman demonstrate the process, considering how well it could be adapted
to his library's need. He decides he will wait until the office
machines convention scheduled to be held in the city in six
weeks before he makes any definite decision. There will be
more processes displayed there and he hopes to get the best.

It is close to five o'clock as he returns to his office. The
state's National Library Week committee is holding an
evaluation meeting that evening at dinner and as a member
he should attend. He gathers up his portable dictaphone, the
controversial book, his hat and coat, and says good night to
his secretary. If he hurries he can get home and get a shave
and a clean shirt before the meeting.

Because of his heavy responsibilities, the head of a growing system may delegate some of his duties to others. An
assistant librarian comes first to mind, who, while functioning
as a second-in-command, may be in charge of all extension
agencies, or of all public services, business operations, personnel, or public relations. The staff in the specific field or
fields assigned to the assistant librarian report directly to
him, thus relieving the librarian of that responsibility and

leaving him free to direct his talent to other areas.

Another common practice is for the librarian to appoint one or more assistants—not assistant librarians—to handle personnel, public relations, and research. These people must have special talents and training in the assigned fields, plus an understanding and knowledge of libraries.

There is debate, both in business and in libraries, as to whether or not such specialists should also be qualified in the business. It is the general opinion now that one who knows the company or the library and has, in addition, ability in the special field, is the best choice, since he relates the product and the business more intelligently to his talent. In other words, a public relations director who is a librarian knows the library, the whys and wherefores of its operations, its goals and aims as well as the unwritten taboos which govern it, and can interpret the institution and its work to the public. A personnel chief who has been a librarian knows what specific jobs require, not only in training but in temperament, the demands they make upon an individual, the intangible rewards in each, and so relates the individual more productively to the position. In research, the librarian knows what to look for where. However, it is important to remember that the qualifications which make these assistants good librarians must be combined with real ability and real knowledge in the field of public relations, or personnel, or research. There are instances in which non-librarians holding such positions in libraries have succeeded brilliantly, but the library director who finds a librarian with a highly developed ability in any of the three fields has struck gold.

Responsibilities in each of these fields will vary with the library, its head, and the talents of the individual. A public relations director will handle the release of information to press, radio, and television; may direct the exhibit program; may be in charge of the library printing; may do all library editing; may write the annual reports and related publications. Because of his knowledge of public reaction, his skill in the visual approach, and his skill with words, he may also assist the librarian in presentations of budgets and building programs to the public. The personnel director's responsibilities will vary also. Among those which may be assigned to him are interviewing job applicants, recommending promotions, keeping all personnel records, preparation of salary schedules for board consideration, the payroll, recruiting, staff training, and orientation. The research assistant will gather the statistics, information, and materials needed by administration and board as a background for action, to answer questionnaires, and generally provide the factual information needed by the library itself in its operations.

The larger the library grows, the more the administrator is removed from direct contact with people using books. He must find his satisfactions in leadership, inspiring others to give that service he believes in; in the development of other's talents—for a good administrator sees potentialities and abilities in those he leads and helps them to develop; in interpretation of the library, its riches, and its needs to the staff, to the board, and to his community. The administrator has long hours, many hard decisions to make, and many personal sacrifices; but in proportion his rewards are great.

Summary

In describing types of work one must always generalize. The result is that any librarian, reading any of the descriptions above, is quite likely to say: "Well! that isn't what I do." Therein lies the great fascination of library work. No job is exactly like anyone else's. A good librarian makes his job through his own abilities and talents. A good community shapes its library—no matter what kind it is. A good administrator molds it in an individual cast to fit the staff, the collection, the traditions, the people.

So can it be with you. As a librarian for children, for young adults, for adults, for servicemen; as a cataloger or a classifier or an acquisitions librarian; as an administrator or a young assistant you can make an important and an individual contribution to the library profession.

EIGHT

Related Jobs

EXPERIENCE HAS BEEN RATED a superior teacher. Once taught by experience you will find several other occupational doors opening to you as a librarian. These you may enter on a part-time basis, your continuing library work serving as a valuable qualification, or you may decide to join one of these related ranks as a full-time member.

Library Education

Library schools frequently turn to practicing librarians to teach specific courses. A children's librarian may teach children's literature; a special librarian, a course in his field; a chief librarian, one in administration; a county library director, one on regional and county library work. They will be chosen for their knowledge, their performance, and their ability to teach.

Their inclusion on the teaching roster has many advantages. The students receive the value of theory with practical applications drawn from the teacher's own experience. He knows what is current and useful in the field as well as what must still be developed and perfected. Many of these developments will come through the ideas and the work of librarians of the future, some of whom sit at desks in library schools today.

Some librarians, recruited thus to teach specific courses, desert the practice of the profession to join the professorial ranks permanently, making their contributions to the professional preparation of their successors a full-time career. To progress in this field they will add studying to their teaching, taking additional credits and seeking advanced degrees, in many cases aiming for a doctorate.

Association Headquarters

For its executive secretaries and for other specific staff jobs the American Library Association draws from the library field. When one joins the ALA headquarters staff, one is working for the profession as a whole. Programs to advance books and reading, the use and development of libraries, and librarianship as a whole must be envisioned, made operable, and then carried forward. The commands of the members in the various divisions must be carried out. The demands for information from both within and without the profession must be answered, counsel given, knowledge shared.

This staff carries on a monumental job which includes annual preparation for two conferences—one at Chicago called the Midwinter Meeting and the annual conference held in June or July in one of the nation's large cities. Publications are put out by several of the divisions, with resulting responsibility at ALA. Any member of the headquarters staff must be able to speak well, to handle a meeting, to write with facility, and to deal with human beings and their problems.

A position at ALA headquarters is not considered a permanent career job. Executive secretaries usually do not plan to stay more than ten years in a position, returning then to practice in the field.

Experience at headquarters is invaluable to you as a librarian for it widens your vision and you learn to think in truly professional terms rather than in the circumscribed language of your own library. It introduces you to the leaders in the field. There are opportunities for travel and great opportunities for serving the profession you have chosen.

Consultant

You have built a new library and remodeled some branches. You have had some background in construction from your preprofessional days and have a natural aptitude for building. Suddenly you discover you are being called on by other librarians facing the experience of building a library for their first and only time. You become a consultant.

This field offers good financial as well as professional returns. Special abilities, training, and experience in many fields can be used to aid other librarians who lack this particular knowledge. Building consultants are frequently employed by architects and library boards. They bring to the employing body a knowledge of design and construction as it relates to libraries, thus combining two fields to serve each other. The special factors governing each job must be considered and reconciled with the over-all wishes and hopes of the builder. This means that no one plan can be imposed on every library. Each one will have its own building budget, each one its own site with attendant considerations as to exposure, access, and construction. Each will have its own patterns of service, its own peculiar history and traditions which must be accommodated in the new structure. The consultant who combines with his own experience a native ability, plus the knowledge gained through professional exchange and through examination of many new libraries, will offer the suggestions and solutions which otherwise might be gained only through bitter experience acquired too late.

There are other types of consultants. Librarians with experience and success in management may be employed to survey a library system. Other common surveys relate to county and regional library use, personnel, branch patterns, management, and building locations.

Finally, librarians with a knowledge of book values are sometimes called upon to evaluate a private library or appraise a collection. In some cases a small number of books may be examined as a public service on the part of the library or as a personal favor on the part of the librarian. A large collection means a serious time-consuming job.

In all consultant work the librarian must first have a real knowledge of the field in which he offers this service. The work means the sacrifice of precious spare time which others devote to home, hobbies, recreation, or personal pursuits if, as in most cases, the consultant does his work in addition to carrying on a full-time library job.

NINE

Other Opportunities in the
Book Field

YOU HAVE BECOME a librarian through
professional education and experience. You love books.

That love plus that experience may also make you a valuable addition to other fields.

Publishing

Some librarians have a talent for writing. The talent
flourishes through constant exposure to the work of other
writers, and a conscious appreciation of their style. Sometimes this ability is used in editing staff or library association
newsletters or in writing articles for professional magazines.
For some it goes farther than that and woos them away from
active librarianship into the field of editing and publishing.

Earlier it was pointed out that children's librarians sometimes leave the ranks to join the juvenile departments of
publishing firms. There are distinguished examples to prove
this is a workable exchange. Librarians in the adult field
have also been known to make the transfer to the book trade,
where their knowledge of the world of books and of what

readers want and need, combined with an appreciation of literary style and quality, make them valuable assets. Here they are still serving libraries and the people who use them by supplying superior products for the shelves.

The editors of the ALA *Bulletin*, the *Library Journal*, and the *Wilson Library Bulletin*, three important periodicals in the profession, are all former librarians. This experience gives them a good grounding in what librarians think, their philosophy, their traditions, and the unwritten laws and customs of the profession. This background, coupled with imagination, a continuing effort to correct things which need improvement, and the ability to put it all into an attractive and readable format will produce a magazine with considerable power and influence.

There are also librarians who have become authors in their own right, authors of real merit and quality. Often they stay in the field, writing their books in the small precious hours away from the library. Lawrence Clark Powell, now director of the William Andrews Clark Memorial Library and head of the new graduate library school at the University of California at Los Angeles, is one of these. In addition to his column in the *Library Journal* called "On the Grindstone" and numerous magazine articles, he has found time to produce such volumes as *The Alchemy of Books, Books West Southwest, A Passion for Books, Books in My Baggage,* and *Recollections of an Ex-Bookseller.*

Sometimes the demands of writing force these librarians to devote full time to it and they leave the job of selecting the right book for the right reader in favor of writing the right books for the right reader. Emma Brock, author of *The Runaway Sardine, Drusilla, The Hen That Kept House* and a host of other children's books, is one of these. She combines her skill at writing with an equal skill in drawing, winning acclaim as an illustrator as well.

Phyllis R. Fenner is a former children's librarian who is the author of *Proof of the Pudding*, and editor or compiler of such books as *Dogs, Dogs, Dogs; Giants and Witches and a Dragon or Two; Adventure, Rare and Magical; Brother Against Brother*, and *Fools and Funny Fellows*. If you have laughed over *Henry Huggins* or *Henry and Ribsy* or *The Real Hole* or *Two Dog Biscuits*, to name just a few of Beverly Cleary's books, you may be interested to know that she, too, was a librarian. A graduate of the University of California at Berkeley and of the school of librarianship at the University of Washington, she was a children's librarian in Yakima, Washington, until she married. She also served as post librarian at the Oakland Army Hospital during World War II.

Book Sales

One of the sources from which librarians are recruited is the bookstore. Sometimes the journey is in the opposite direction and a librarian leaves the profession for the business world. The knowledge and training of a librarian makes him valuable as a publisher's representative. Nor is it unusual for a librarian to go into the world that produces encyclopedias.

In all these areas the librarian's acquaintance with the wide field of books and their use and enjoyment by people is an invaluable asset. Bookstores need salespeople who know the whole range of literature and who can select the right one for a particular customer. For a librarian this is only "doin' what comes naturally."

A publisher's representative will call upon librarians and meet them at conferences. If he is a former librarian his enthusiasm for books and his knowledge of their use by libraries makes him well qualified to introduce new titles to other librarians. In the same way, the recruits to the field of encyclopedia publishing and sales know what librarians value in the way of arrangement, accuracy, and timeliness. They know how to interpret library needs and how, in turn, to show librarians where these needs have been met.

Indexing

The library world depends upon many indexes and catalogs which appear at regular intervals. There are guides to periodicals so that the reader can find a particular magazine article or locate material in periodicals on a given subject. There are catalogs of published books which enable one to locate bibliographical information about old and new publications as well as those in particular subject fields. There are indexes to newspapers and compilations of book reviews. Some of these are general in their coverage; others are devoted to definite subject areas. To keep these invaluable tools in production, serving the librarian, the scholar, and the researcher as well as the average man, capable people are needed who understand the use of indexes and catalogs, who know how to make them, who are familiar with the subject headings as well as the workings of the human mind when looking for a subject. It is natural that publishers turn to the library world to find such people.

In leaving the practicing field of librarianship for that of publishing, book sales, writing, or indexing, librarians simply choose another way to serve the people who use libraries, by producing more books and making them available and accessible to the reader. When they are capable and well qualified, both their present and their former professions profit.

Not a small byproduct of this exchange is the valuable contribution they can make in promoting public understanding of libraries. Speaking as people who know by experience, they can represent to their new world the value, the contribution, the unique place of libraries in the world, as well as their needs and their problems. By the very fact of being intelligent, outstanding, and able people in their new field, they increase the stature of librarians.

TEN

If You Cannot Get a Library Degree

EVER SINCE the day she got her first library card, writing her name with careful, practiced strokes, Mary Beth had wanted to be a librarian. When she was in grade school she stopped at the library every night on her way to the skating rink down the block, or—in summer—to the tennis court. Her room was decorated with summer honor reading certificates, mounted a little awkwardly but with tender pride, in cheap frames. In high school she had been first a member, then president, of the library club.

In her senior year, Mary Beth began to realize that it would be impossible for her to go to college. Her father's salary could not be stretched far enough. In fact, that salary would need the help of what Mary Beth could make if her brothers and sisters were to have the happy high school days she had enjoyed. But surely, she thought, there must be some place in a library where she could work.

Mary Beth talked to the school librarian and also to the head of the branch library that she had used so faithfully ever since she could read. Acting upon their counsel she registered for the civil service examinations for junior clerk and for junior library aid. Fortunately for Mary Beth an

exam was scheduled for September. That was not too long
to wait. The summer flew by while she studied for her exam,
swam in the sunny blue waters of the lake, and earned a
really creditable sum, she thought, working at the corner
drugstore. Exam time came and with a room full of other
applicants she bit at her pencil, chewed her tongue, and wrote
answers.

Mary Beth knew that when the exams were graded a list
would be made in order of rank from the top grade to the
lowest. As vacancies occurred, the top applicant on the list
would have first chance at the job. If he did not want it, he
would waive his chance and it would go to the next on the
list. Occasionally this order would vary a bit if there were
veterans on the list who receive credit for their period in the
armed services.

What excitement there was the day Mary Beth was noti-
fied that there was a vacancy at the library for a junior library aid! She made an appointment to see Mrs. Jamison, the
library's personnel officer the next day, then fell to worrying
as to which dress she should wear. She consulted anxiously
with her mother. Did she think she should wear her new black
flats or her heeled shoes, which were old, but would look nice
if they were polished?

Finally, all decisions were made with the help of the entire
family and Mary Beth set off, inwardly quaking but seeming
as poised and cool as her younger brothers and sisters thought
she really was. The library looked big and busy to her. She
asked her way to the offices. Mrs. Jamison greeted her cheer-
ily and soon had her comfortably talking about her experiences in the high school library and the different kinds of
work she had done during her vacations. In a while they got
around to the job for which Mary Beth was applying. It

was in one of the branch libraries, rather far from where Mary Beth lived, but in an interesting neighborhood. Mary Beth would be assigned the routine clerical work. Among her duties, Mrs. Jamison said, would be to charge and discharge books. Mary Beth knew what this meant from her work in the school library club. She wriggled with pleasure, seeing herself sitting at the desk coolly stamping books, smiling at the people who were taking them out, gently pointing out that this one was overdue.

She came out of her dream to find Mrs. Jamison going on down the list of duties.

"You will arrange, count, and file the circulation—do you know the Dewey decimal classification?"

Mary Beth nodded, making a mental note to dash home and study it thoroughly.

Mrs. Jamison was going on:

"You will take applications, write overdue notices, check in new magazines, and answer the telephone. Of course," she added, "any questions about books or which require reference work directed to you over the telephone or the desk, you turn over to the librarian. But then, why don't I take you to extension headquarters and let you learn the rest there."

Mrs. Jamison took Mary Beth through a maze of stairs and halls (later she would know these as well as the upstairs passage at home) and brought her out in the office of the head of all the branches. There she learned more about her job. She would prepare and file pamphlets and clippings, get magazines ready for circulation, mend torn books, process books ready for binding and for discard, mount pictures and clippings, stamp various forms with the branch identification, sort the date due cards with a Keysort process, help to shelve books and to revise the shelving, arrange catalog cards, help

set up exhibits and displays, assist with the inventory, pack
and unpack the delivery boxes.

Mary Beth's eyes grew rounder and rounder.

Miss Benjamin smiled.

"Don't worry," she said. "You'll learn one thing at a time.
It sounds like a lot now but soon you'll feel as if you have
been doing it all your life."

She told Mary Beth that she would have a training period
at the central library before going to the branch. Mary Beth
would report the next morning for it.

Before she left the library, Mary Beth returned to Mrs.
Jamison, made out the necessary employment forms, and was
given information about her employment status.

"Just think," she told her admiring family, "I get a check
every other Friday, and I have eleven working days vacation
and I can have sick leave after I'm there six months"—she
started to giggle—"and I get a pension when I retire!"

After her training period, Mary Beth went to the branch
library. She knew that she would work under the direction
of the branch librarian and a senior library aid. There were
other librarians in the branch, one working with adults and
the other with the children. She reveled in being with books
all day and worked hard to see that her report after six
months of probation was a favorable one.

Mary Beth soon learned that there were many kinds of jobs
for clerks and aids in a large library. Some of those she met
worked in agencies that had mechanical charging and, where
Mary Beth stamped the card of a book that was going out,
they pressed a button and took its picture. They read film to
find out what books were overdue. There was more to the job
than that, she knew, just as there was more to hers than the
pencil and stamp.

There were aids who assisted in special subject departments. For instance, there was one in music who processed records and sheet music for circulation. One of the aids in the art department spent the bulk of her time clipping, marking, mounting, and filing pictures. There were clerks who ran the offices of the library officials, typing their correspondence, filing letters, making appointments, and doing similar tasks related to any business office.

On her trips to the central library Mary Beth became well acquainted with a short, pretty blonde girl who worked in the catalog department. Her work was completely different from Mary Beth's for she devoted her time to producing catalog cards. Thousands were needed for the library's many files. She took Mary Beth in to see the machines she used, taking visible and rightful pride in the quality of her work.

Mary Beth went to work in a large public library system. Clerical positions exist in all libraries, however—large and small, special, school, college, and research. Just as in the professional field, a clerical job in a small operation tends to include a wider range of duties and to become more specialized as the size of the operation increases.

One of the trends in libraries which will become more marked each year is the sharper and sharper division between clerical and professional duties. Because of the costs of library service, it is important to keep high standards of professional service and at the same time keep budgets within bounds. One of the ways to do this is to make it possible for librarians to do professional work only—to use their time for the guidance of readers, for reference and research, for book selection, for building a closer relationship between the library user and the library materials he needs. This will mean that a competent, capable clerical staff is needed to keep the routines functioning smoothly.

Based on present studies, the division suggested by **ALA** in the public library standards is a proportion of one-third professional staff to two-thirds nonprofessional.

In its guide to minimum standards for public library service, the American Library Association states that non-professional positions fall into three classes: administrative, which includes the business operations and routine; clerical, which also includes paging and shelving; and maintenance. While they may require specialized training and demand clerical ability of a high order, they do not require a broad knowledge of books and the theory of librarianship.

Better operations can be achieved through these sharper distinctions. Librarians make better librarians than they do typists, stenographers, or clerks. People trained in these skills do the job better and faster.

More recognition of the importance of the clerical side of the operation has been seen in the establishment of more avenues of promotion for the clerical staff. Business offices, circulation departments, processing rooms—these are a few of the areas where the head of the operation may be from the clerical ranks.

Pay for nonprofessional work should conform to standards in the community, similar work under similar conditions being worth the same rate at the library as it would be in any other business.

A Word of Caution

If you really have your heart set on becoming a librarian you will not be happy in a clerical position. While, like Mary Beth, you may be thrilled at the outset to be in a library, surrounded by books and working with readers, you will find yourself circumscribed as your experience grows. The distinctions between professional and nonprofessional work will fence you in. There can be no advancement for you in the world of books. You will long to be involved in reference service, to be concerned with the selection of books, to give counsel on reading problems, to bring books and readers together. If you have this urge, the satisfaction of making the library's operations function smoothly, of providing the groundwork on which the librarian builds, will not satisfy you for long.

You should look on a clerical position as the means to an end. In other words use it to provide the money you need for your college education and for library school. This is a hard road but has been traveled by many librarians before you. There are work-study plans available where by an arrangement between the library school and the library itself you can set up a schedule that divides your time between classes and work. Individual libraries not involved in a formal work-study program have many times arranged a worker's schedule so that he could take courses at the same time.

While you are studying and when you finally get those two degrees and take your place as a professional librarian you will find that your knowledge of clerical operations, learned on the job, will stand you in good stead. In class your library background helps you to see at once the practical application of some of the theories you are learning. When you enter the professional ranks your clerical experience will make you a better supervisor and a more understanding librarian.

ELEVEN

Through Tomorrow's Door

WE ARE IN THE 1960's. A librarian sits
down at his desk in the morning. In the next 60 seconds
2,000 pages of print will be published throughout the world.
Every minute of every hour this happens. If that librarian
could devote his full time to reading everything, he would
be a billion pages behind at the end of the year. How much
farther behind will the librarian fall who attempts to order,
process, index, and use these materials to serve the public.

Even now, from 50,000 to 100,000 technical journals are
published in 60 different languages with new ones appearing
at the rate of two a day. No wonder special librarians particularly are staggered at the thought of producing from
this monumental pile of print the information wanted by
a scientist or researcher.

Conscious of this inability of mankind to cope unaided with
the surging flood of print his own inventions have let loose,
industry is working on systems for documentation and information retrieval. Magnetic tape, punched cards, micro-
photography, computers—all of these and more can be
turned to the aid of the library user. Special libraries, perhaps, have made the first advances in this field since many of

them are financed by private funds and since, also, they often serve critical programs such as space exploration and atomic research.

Library prophets, such as Marjorie Griffin, writing in "The Library of Tomorrow," published in the *Library Journal* of April 15, 1962, expresses the hope that soon mechanical equipment will be able:

> to catalog information—even abstract it;
>
> to solve the critical storage problem;
>
> to take the patron's request, analyze it, search for and retrieve the information which answers it;
>
> to meet the needs of the scientist in advance by anticipating them and selecting the necessary information;
>
> to answer several queries at once, something the busy librarian has tried to do but not with the dispassionate self-possession of a machine;
>
> to take a patron's educational background, reading level, age and other pertinent factors, match them with his request for reading material and produce a printed bibliography suitable to the individual, or even to serve him directly with the document he needs;
>
> and finally, to conduct a search just as the librarian does now, but if the answer cannot be found to transmit the question automatically to a regional center.

There are many systems of documentation and information retrieval now in use and it is to be expected that more and more will be produced. Information can be stored in a variety of ways. Edge-notched cards are already familiar to many laymen as they see them used in banks, department stores, and other everyday operations. Another kind of a card is named the "Peekaboo." It is searched by using a light behind selected parts of the complete file.

Several systems use microfilm. There is the punched aperture card which holds a microfilm picture. Another system imprints an indexing code photographically on reels next to the microphoto of the original document. Information is searched on the reels by machines that "read" the index code. Then there are minicards which differ from the preceding in the fact that the microfilm is cut in tiny pieces and handled like cards.

Another company has a system which reproduces 10,000 pages on a glass plate one foot square. This is used with equipment which will select a page on demand and print an enlarged photo of it. This depends upon an index separately produced. Another type of card is a three-inch plastic one on which information is stored magnetically. Three hundred of these cards can be searched in a minute.

Machine abstracting is possible through IBM's 704 data processing computer. According to Robert Kingery, chief of the Preparations Division of the New York Public Library:

It doesn't take much imagination to see the day when punched tape will be produced as a part of the composing process and that machine editing, indexing and subject analysis will be upon us. . . . The 704 can contain original texts, abstracts and bibliographies. It can itself make the last two.

Remington Rand's famous UNIVAC has demonstrated some of its library uses. It has been programmed with the sections of the Great Books of the Western World. Supposing a man wanted to know what Aristotle had said on the subject of government; the query would be fed into the machine and in seconds the answer would appear. This machine has also been used to produce the personalized bibliographies mentioned earlier.

In this library which is developing around us now, translating machines and teaching machines will be common equipment. So will television screens. The library user may sit in a cubicle and have information he needs flashed on a closed-circuit television screen. Neither need he be limited by the resources of his own library. Instead of going through the time-consuming process of the present interlibrary loan system, his request can be flashed automatically to the library having the information he needs, and back will come the answer via television. Less dramatic perhaps will be the use of closed-circuit television by branches in a library system. Their patron's requests will be transmitted to the central headquarters in minutes, the reply flashing back on the screen.

It may be that the reader will no longer receive overdue notices in the future because he will no longer borrow a book. Instead it will be cheaper and easier to reproduce the material he needs from some type of microfilmed collection, the patron going home with a print of it.

Even now, libraries are using reader-printers on which they search for the information needed on microfilm. Once the information is found, the patron can either read it on the screen or, by dropping a coin in the slot, receive a printed copy which comes forth from the machine at his touch of a button much as the genie appeared when Aladdin rubbed his lamp.

The Librarian and the Machine

You may be thinking, "Why should I spend five years in college and several thousand dollars studying librarianship only to find myself replaced by a machine?"

If you are, you may take heart from this statement made by J. R. Blanchard, librarian of the University of California Library at Davis, in the *Library Journal* for May 1, 1959.

There now exist in certain intelligence centers information finding machines which represent a great advance in the development and organization of knowledge. Based almost entirely on the use of anthropoidal neuron centers, plus the ancillary use of spatial-optical relationships and digital manipulation by homonoids, this amazing machine may soon make obsolete the unsophisticated use of electronic data processing machines.

This machine, unfortunately, is often called a "card catalog," a Victorian term now quite meaningless and without any semantic validity. Examples of this "machine" may be seen in almost any library.

Elaborate processes of documentation and information retrieval cannot be adopted wholesale by every library. Outlay for the equipment is tremendous. That is one reason for the emphasis upon automatic transmission of information from regional centers. In that way many widely scattered agencies can realize returns from one investment.

Secondly, there are operations where the present conventional tools and human searching are faster and cheaper than a data processing machine or digital computer. You do not gas up the power mower to cut a few nasturtiums. A homemaker does not preheat the oven to toast a single slice of bread. Librarians, like businessmen, must have an eye to the economics of an operation and structure it to suit the situation.

Thirdly, as Francis Bello, writing in *Fortune* magazine September 1960, says: "Properly used, the conventional tools of library scholarship are extremely effective—up to a point. It is true, too, that machines can retrieve nothing that was not thoughtfully indexed and abstracted in the first place."

Librarians are trained to index and to abstract thoughtfully. Their work with the individual library user makes them perceptive as to the needs of human minds, the way people ask for things (which sometimes has no apparent connection with what they want), the key or code words which pop first into mind when pursuing a subject. Being trained to indexing, they should be receptive to the new theories of analyzing language and coding ideas.

This does not mean that librarians can sit back complacently and say the revolution in information storage and retrieval will not affect them. Far from it. They are already on the firing line and some do not yet realize it. Libraries—even small ones—are using microfilms, microcards, and their accompanying readers. Reproduction of materials in the library for the patron to take with him has become more highly developed and simpler with use of such processes as Xerox, Verifax, Thermofax, and 3 M's reader-printer.

In Chapter Six, there was reference to a statement by Dr. Trump who said the school librarian of the future would be an expert on the technology of instruction. Already school librarians are working with translating machines, teaching machines, and other new devices, just as special librarians are forging ahead in data processing and automated information retrieval. Business and industry have shown some scorn for the term "librarian," substituting "information scientist" for it. Only by taking the lead in adapting the new systems to their own use can librarians hold on to the profession they have chosen. They have much to give in this field; by using their gifts intelligently and promptly they can help to direct the revolution in research methods so that it makes the greatest gains for the most people.

Training for the New Systems

Undoubtedly, library schools will place more and more emphasis on the areas of documentation and information retrieval in order to keep pace with developments in this field. Western Reserve University in Cleveland established a Center for Documentation and Communication Research in 1955. This was the first such center to be connected with a school of library science.

It has four major objectives which are listed in the library school catalog:

1. To conduct research programs for the definition of techniques and principles underlying the organization of recorded information for effective use by the businessman, the professional man, the scientist, the scholar, the administrator, and the technician;

2. To improve the accessibility of recorded information (on a contract basis) for industrial, governmental, and educational organizations through the identification and establishment of bases for synthesis where fragmentation now exists;

3. To offer students in the library school not only the opportunity for study of information systems in operation, individual research laboratory experience, and advanced seminars, but also the educational advantages of contact with national leaders in the field of documentation;

4. To establish a demonstration mechanized literature exploitation center.

The man who wrote that knew what he was talking about and, from that knowledge, stated it in the most descriptive terms. To the student contemplating a library career it may read more like Greek, unless it is examined carefully. This careful reading shows that the center investigates the methods and principles by which the flood of recorded information can be organized so that those who need it may use it to their advantage. It also, by contract, seeks to make recorded information more available to industry, government, and education through searching out and establishing principles for combining what are now scattered fragments. It offers to library school students a chance to study the various informational systems at first hand, to carry on individual research with the new methods through laboratory work and through seminars. More, since it is pioneering in this field, the center draws national leaders in documentation. Acquaintance with these experts is a valuable contribution to the students' experience and knowledge. Last, the center is a continuing demonstration of the place of machines in utilizing literature.

Among courses offered at Western Reserve is Language Engineering, which considers language as a system of symbols conveying ideas; its place in the formation of indexes and classification systems; codes and artificial language in the use of punched cards and electronic equipment; and the employment of the theory of information and of games in originating codes and machine languages.

Another course, called Machine Literature Searching, reviews recently developed methods and equipment as well as those now being designed for the analysis, storage, correlation, and retrieval of recorded information. The systems are considered from the way in which they can be used practically in various fields, and emphasis is placed on coordinating the new methods with the more conventional indexes and

classification systems. In this course the student sees some of
the systems and coding techniques demonstrated.

Information Processing on Computers is a course which
offers a historical review of computer developments, and their
practical use. Problems are run on the GE-225 computer.
Information centers here and abroad which employ mechanical or electronic aids are considered in a course on specialized information centers; the activities of the Western
Reserve Center for Documentation and Communication Research are examined in detail. Administration, training, and
cost accounting are included along with specialized problems.

Students who undertake special research projects in this
field have the GE-225 computer available.

This is a sampling of the type of course offered to students
who choose this area of study. As advances are made, more
and different courses will be developed to keep pace with
them. Other schools will include more courses in their curriculum to prepare the student for the new library world.

Meantime here is a field of exploration for the newcomer as
challenging as any which lay before the young pioneer who
donned buckskin and breeches and headed for the great
Western plains a century ago. Here are trackless forests
filled not with Indians and animals but with ideas and information. These must be found and brought into order. Here,
too, for the inventive and curious mind is an opportunity to
join those who are experimenting with mechanical means to
aid the stalking of ideas.

Epilogue

Exciting though they may seem because of their novelty,
machines alone will not make the library of tomorrow. Always

a library will be *people* seeking information, seeking knowledge, seeking ideas. Always there must be other people—librarians—to see that the seekers find the gold.

Films, slides, pictures, microfilm, tape and the many more new methods men of the future will find to transmit ideas will be utilized by librarians but always, before the film or the tape, must come the word, the word in print.

Libraries are many things to many people—to some, a storehouse of knowledge; to some, the people's university; to others, a refuge, an ivory tower; to still others, an arsenal of ideas. In a democratic society, one which depends upon an educated citizenry, a library is not a luxury. It is the place of independent study where the child, educated by a national system of private and public schools, continues his education as a man. There is little advantage in legislating a literate electorate into existence if that literacy is not put to use.

Not only does national and international understanding and harmony depend upon this continuing pursuit of truth; the harmony of man's interior spirit must depend upon it also. Today's library, whether it be labeled school, college, or public, is the fortress of the individual. There, away from mass persuasion and popular pressures, he may read, examine, ponder, and judge.

Tomorrow's librarian can travel a glory road, fighting to make libraries open to peoples of all colors, stumping the country to get books to all who need and want them, resisting pressures to subvert the purpose of his particular library and assuming leadership in the thoughtful builders of the coming community.

APPENDIX

Library Schools

CALIFORNIA

School of Librarianship
University of California
Berkeley 4, Calif.
Established 1919. Degree: M.L.S.

School of Library Service
University of California
Los Angeles 24, Calif.
Established 1960. Degree: M.L.S.

School of Library Science
University of Southern California
University Park, Los Angeles 7, Calif.
Established 1936. Degree: M.S. in L.S.

COLORADO

School of Librarianship
University of Denver
Denver 10, Colo.
Established 1931. Degree: M.A.

FLORIDA

Library School
Florida State University
Tallahassee, Fla.
Established 1947. Degrees: M.A. and M.S.

GEORGIA
    School of Library Service
    Atlanta University
    Atlanta, Ga.
    Established 1941. Degrees: M.S. in L.S.

    Division of Librarianship
    Emory University
    Atlanta 22, Ga.
    Established 1905. Degrees: M.A., M.L'ship, M.S.

ILLINOIS
    Department of Library Science
    Rosary College
    River Forest, Ill.
    Established 1930. Degree: M.A. in L.S.

    Graduate Library School
    University of Chicago
    Chicago 37, Ill.
    Established 1928. Degree: M.A.

    Graduate School of Library Science
    University of Illinois
    Urbana, Ill.
    Established 1893. Degree: M.S.

INDIANA
    Division of Library Science
    Indiana University
    Bloomington, Ind.
    Established 1949. Degree: M.A.

KENTUCKY
    Department of Library Science
    University of Kentucky
    Lexington, Ky.
    Established 1933. Degrees: M.A., M.S. in L.S.

LOUISIANA
Library School
University Station
Louisiana State University
Baton Rouge 3, La.
Established 1931. Degree: M.S.

MASSACHUSETTS
School of Library Science
Simmons College
Boston 15, Mass.
Established 1902. Degree: M.S.

MICHIGAN
Department of Library Science
University of Michigan
Ann Arbor, Mich.
Established 1926. Degree: M.A. in L.S.

Department of Librarianship
Western Michigan University
Kalamazoo, Mich.
Established 1945. Degree: M.A.

MINNESOTA
Library School
University of Minnesota
Minneapolis 14, Minn.
Established 1928. Degree: M.A.

NEW JERSEY
Graduate School of Library Service
Rutgers University
New Brunswick, N. J.
Established 1953. Degree: M.L.S.

NEW YORK
    School of Library Service
    Columbia University
    New York 27, N. Y.
Established 1887. Degree: M.S.

    Library School
    Pratt Institute
    Brooklyn 5, N. Y.
Established 1890. Degree: M.L.S.

    School of Library Science
    Syracuse University
    Syracuse 10, N. Y.
Established 1908. Degree: M.S.

NORTH CAROLINA
    School of Library Science
    University of North Carolina
    Chapel Hill, N. C.
Established 1931. Degree: M.S. in L.S.

OKLAHOMA
    School of Library Science
    University of Oklahoma
    Norman, Okla.
Established 1929. Degrees: M.A. in L.S., M.L.S.

OHIO
    School of Library Science
    Western Reserve University
    Cleveland 6, Ohio
Established 1904. Degree: M.S. in L.S.

PENNSYLVANIA
    Carnegie Library School
    Carnegie Institute of Technology
    Pittsburgh 13, Pa.
(Closed June 1962) Degree: M.L.S.

Graduate School of Library Science
Drexel Institute of Technology
Philadelphia 4, Pa.
Established 1891. Degree: M.S. in L.S.

TENNESSEE
Peabody Library School
George Peabody School for Teachers
Nashville 5, Tenn.
Established 1928. Degree: M.A.

TEXAS
School of Library Science
Texas Woman's University
Denton, Tex.
Established 1929. Degrees: M.A., M.L.S.

Graduate School of Library Science
University of Texas
Austin 12, Tex.
Established 1948. Degree: M.L.S.

WASHINGTON
School of Librarianship
University of Washington
Seattle 5, Wash.
Established 1911. Degree: M. of L'ship.

WISCONSIN
Library School
University of Wisconsin
Madison 6, Wis.
Established 1906. Degrees: M.A. and M.S.

DISTRICT OF COLUMBIA
Department of Library Science
Catholic University of America
Washington 17, D. C.
Established 1938. Degree: M.S. in L.S.

CANADA*
    Library School
    McGill University
    Montreal 2, Canada
    Established 1927. Degree: B.L.S.

    Library School
    Ontario College of Education
    Toronto 5, Canada
    Established 1928. Degree: B.L.S.

* Both Canadian library schools offer a basic program at the fifth year level which leads to a professional *bachelor's* degree accredited under the standards adopted by the ALA Council on July 13, 1951.

INDEX

ABOUT THE AUTHOR

Sarah L. Wallace was born in Kansas City, Missouri. When she was a small child her family moved to Minneapolis and she attended high school there. She received her A.B. at the College of St. Catherine, and her degree in library science at the library school there.

"Upon receiving my library degree," she writes, "I went to work in the reference department of the Minneapolis Public Library, with short stints in a junior high school and in a neighborhood branch. At the College of St. Catherine I taught in the library school—adolescent literature, library administration, library publicity, public relations, and community relations. Since 1942 I have been engaged in library public relations and administration, now serving as public relations officer of the Minneapolis Public Library.

"Art and writing have been major hobbies and at one time I was all for making a career of one or the other or both. Now I combine them a good deal with my daily work and with free lance assignments. An annual December job is the design and production of Christmas cards for myself and a few friends."

Miss Wallace was at the ALA headquarters in Chicago for some months in 1960; and was also part-time instructor at the

College of St. Catherine. She has conducted seminars and workshops or served on the staff of special institutes in Iowa City, the University of San Francisco, and the College of Santa Barbara.

Her writings have appeared in the ALA *Bulletin*, *Library Journal*, *Wilson Library Bulletin*, and other magazines, as well as *American Home*, *Catholic World*, and *Mademoiselle*. Her other books include *Patrons Are People*, *Promotion Ideas for Public Libraries*, and *Friends of the Library*, all published by ALA. She illustrated the first two herself.